PRAISE FOR TEACHING WILL

"*Teaching Will* sings with honesty, adventure, humility and humor. Only some-one who loves Shakespeare would dare to do what Ms. Ryane did and dare to write about it. The book is a joy."

—HELEN HUNT, Oscar, Golden Globe, and Emmy winner

"In her lively memoir reaching back to moments in her own acting career, Ryane manages both to be funny and not take herself too seriously, though the respect she instilled in the children is remarkable: respect for her direction, for each other, and for the genius of Shakespeare."

—PUBLISHERS WEEKLY

"Hilarious, tender, and instructive, Mel Ryane's very personal story of teaching a cast of eight-year-olds that they can be Shakespearean actors is as moving and delightful a performance as any on a stage. She deserves our standing ovation."

—TOM HAYDEN, author and teacher

"I was completely caught up in Mel Ryane's story of a theatre artist who dis-covers a metaphor for her life's journey while teaching third-, fourth-, and fifth-graders the joy of theatre and storytelling through the words of William Shakespeare. I absolutely loved it!"

—JUDY KAYE, Tony Award and Drama Desk Award winner

"Inspiring, funny, touching, and rewarding. The book is a great read for actors, teachers, parents, and young adults. Mel Ryane's insights are a lesson on how receptive kids can be when they have a new world opened up to them."

—MARK MOSES, Screen Actors Guild Award winner

"It was truly magical. Mel Ryane humorously and poignantly reveals her dance with illusion, delusion, and reality while chronicling her journey to open the world of Shakespeare to grade-schoolers. I laughed out loud. Then I cried."

—CHRISTINE ESTABROOK, Drama Desk Award and Obie Award winner

"Oh! For a muse of fire that would ascend the brightest heaven of invention! What a terrific story, funny and brave! Shakespeare gives his actors a glimpse into their humanity, teaches them patience, and fosters their courage. Mel Ryane does the same for her wayward students, and they return the favor. Bravissima!"

—LEN CARIOU, Tony Award and Drama Desk Award winner,
Member of the Theater Hall of Fame

"All Mel Ryane's strutting and fretting signifies a great deal to the budding thespians in her charge. A beautifully calibrated memoir told with great heart and humor. Brava!"

—BARBARA WILLIAMS, Gemini Award winner

MEL RYANE

TEACHING WILL

WHAT SHAKESPEARE AND 10 KIDS GAVE
ME THAT HOLLYWOOD COULDN'T

For William

without whom my life would be ridic u l o u s

Published by Familius LLC, www.familius.com

Familius books are available at special discounts for bulk purchases for sales promotions, family, or corporate use. Special editions, including personalized covers, excerpts of existing books, or books with corporate logos, can be created in large quantities for special needs. For more information, contact Premium Sales at 559-876-2170 or email specialmarkets@familius.com

Library of Congress Catalog-in-Publication Data

2014937612

pISBN 978-1-939629-23-4
eISBN 978-1-939629-43-2

Printed in the United States of America

Edited by Jasmine Ye
Cover Design by David Miles
Book Design by Maggie Wickes

10 9 8 7 6 5 4 3 2 1

First Edition

This is a tale of lessons.
Lessons hard-fought, sometimes painful, and often embarrassing.
Within the confines of an elementary schoolroom, one expects to find a group of students learning. One expects to see an adult urging and encouraging the exchange of information into and out of these young minds.

Alas, the first lesson: beware of expectations.

ME, *an idealist*

WILLIAM, *a smart rock*

MARIN, *a provocateur*

DANA, *a Gulliver*

STELLA, *a whiner*

CARLA, *a round, shy one*

ANNA, *a loner in a pink boa*

MILES, *a boy*

JENNIFER, *a beauty*

CANDACE, *a Bottom twin*

JORDANNA, *a twin of many parts*

GRACE, *a Puck of a girl*

REGINA, *a historian*

DANIEL, *another boy*

AZRA, *a traveler*

ATTENDING TEACHERS; TOWNSPEOPLE; PARENTS

SCENE: *Los Angeles, a public elementary school*]

THE CONTENTS

CHAPTER I

THE SCHOOL OF SOFT KNOCKS

Hath homely age th' alluring beauty took
From my poor cheek? . . .
Are my discourses dull? Barren my wit?

The Comedy of Errors, Act II, Scene I

D id you know him?"

"Oh, no. William Shakespeare lived over four hundred and forty years ago."

"Yeah, but did you know him?"

Twelve sets of eyes scope me out as I sit in front of them. Two boys and ten girls from the third, fourth, and fifth grades. Russell Crowe, Colosseum . . . I get it. These tiny Romans are salivating over my certain death. My mouth trembles as I smile, slapping on a sunny disposition.

"No . . . sad to say, I've never actually met the man."

It's a lame joke, and they don't give an inch, not a flicker of politeness to ease my awkwardness. I sputter out a few coughs and clear my throat. Tough crowd.

"What do you think people didn't have four hundred and forty years ago?" I ask.

"Shoes?"

"No, they had shoes."

"Milk?"

"No, they had milk. You know what they didn't have four hundred and forty years ago? Game Boys, PSPs, DVDs, and iPods."

The entire room groans.

"Hey! Hey, Miss!" An arm waves to get my attention. It's attached to a skinny girl bouncing up and down.

"Yes?"

"Are you famous?"

"No . . . no, I'm definitely not famous. What's your name?"

"Marin. What TV shows and movies are you in?" It's impossible to miss the challenge in Marin's voice.

At a parent-teacher meeting a few weeks ago, I handed out brochures advertising the Shakespeare Club, my after-school program. The pamphlet included a brief biography mentioning my career as an actor and my work as a dialogue and acting coach. There was no mention of time spent as a public school teacher because I am not, nor have I ever been, one.

"It's true, Marin, I was an actor for a long time in the theatre and in a few movies and television shows, but I stopped doing that a while ago. Actually, before you were even born." An annoying bead of sweat trickles down the inside of my arm. I clutch my elbow close, hoping the wetness doesn't show.

Marin's hair is pulled tight into braids. She tilts her head, chews the inside of her cheek, and keeps me in her eyeline.

"What TV shows were you in?"

"You wouldn't know them—"

"Yeah, I would. What ones?"

God, give it up! I want to scream, but you shouldn't scream at children. That's never a good idea, and certainly not at the very first meeting. I release a long sigh.

"What are you in?" is the most dreaded question for actors. It stands as a painful reminder that one may not be "in" anything at the moment. I haven't had to answer this question in a long time because I'd walked away from my acting career ten years earlier. Marin is picking at my scab.

"Here's what I'll do, Marin," I say, looking into her brown eyes. "One day I'll bring you pictures of me acting in some of William Shakespeare's plays."

Marin shakes her head and shrugs.

The roll call list in my hand has become a little damp. I wish it were a picture of me in an episode of *Friends*, but it isn't. It's a list of children I don't know.

I set the paper on the carpeted floor and slide my sweaty palms down the lap of my jeans. *Pull yourself together.* They're just kids gathered on the storytime risers in the library of Arden Street Elementary School in Los Angeles. I check out the room and take comfort in the door. The door is my friend. I could leave any old time I want to, right out that sucker.

There are also, of course, filled shelves. Books, a stuffed figure, more books, and another stuffed figure. Curious George and one of Max's monsters from *Where the Wild Things Are*. Stellaluna the bat and a stunned gray rat from the pages of *Harry Potter*. And there's Captain Underpants, a superhero clad in tighty-whities. I wish I were running a program about his adventures and not the likes of Hamlet with his complicated life.

What am I doing here? What was I thinking? How did this happen?

Wandering the aisles of Staples, I'd picked out notebooks. Blue ones and red ones, green ones and orange ones. I'd filled a cart with HB yellow pencils and packages of colored pens. I then carefully sharpened each pencil to a pointy tip with my brand-new, battery-operated sharpener that made a happy whizzing noise. I made sure each eraser was firmly attached, looking like a tiny, pink pillbox hat. This was going to be good. This is what I was meant to do.

I went to the Santa Monica library and checked out an atlas with maps of England, as well as books about Elizabeth I and her dad Henry VIII and books filled with pictures of Shakespeare's home in Stratford-upon-Avon and the Globe Theatre in London. At the computer, I printed out reams of facts about what the Elizabethans wore and ate and did for fun.

I was ready. I told the principal I would accept only twenty-five students, first come, first served. Twenty-five and not one more.

At home, I prepared. I meditated, breathing deep. I hummed to warm up my voice. I did exactly what I had done for years to get ready for a performance onstage. This is what I knew.

Here in the library, my books, papers, notebooks, and pens are stacked on the floor beside me. I bend down and touch them to make sure they're ready for their entrances. I sit up, fold my hands, and smile at these twelve children. Twelve kids rounded up by the enthusiastic principal. I was frigging lucky we didn't get close to twenty-five.

"My name is Mel Ryane, but you can call me Mel. I'm kinda lousy at remembering names, but I promise that over the next few meetings, I will learn all of yours."

Tap, tap, tap. I turn to the knocks coming from the locked library door.

"I'm sorry, just let me get this." I race to the door and open it, but no one is there. I zip back to my chair, not wanting to lose my momentum or the kids' attention.

"So, here's the thing. This is the first ever meeting of the first ever Shakespeare Club at Arden Street Elementary."

"Miss, uh . . . um . . ."

"Mel, just call me Mel."

"Do you mean . . . are we making history?"

I check my list, trying to match the name to the girl. "You are . . . ?"

"Regina."

Regina is a thin eight-year-old with long, dark hair, dark eyes, and delicate features.

"Yes, exactly, you are making history, Regina," I bubble, "like William Shakespeare made history with his writing."

Are we making history? That's rich. That's adorable.

"Can I go to the bathroom?"

I look again at the list and take a stab. "Dana?"

"No," she frowns, disgusted. "I'm Carla." Carla is also eight and as round as she is tall.

"Sorry, Carla." How was I supposed to know that? "Um . . . yeah, sure, go ahead."

"Me too?" asks a girl beside Carla.

This is happening too fast. "Are you . . . I don't know . . . what's your name?"

"Graciella," she answers in a small voice, "but you can call me Grace."

"Is that what you like to be called?"

"I like Grace."

I make a note. *Prefers to be called Grace.* Grace is the same age as Carla. And I can see right away they're best friends. Their proximity on the risers is so close that they appear physically attached.

"Okay, sure, go." I don't want to make a mistake with these children. I certainly don't want to cause burst bladders.

The two girls race off. I return my attention to the others.

"Please, close your eyes." I shut my own eyes to show them what I mean. "Take a deep breath . . . hold it . . . hold it . . . hold it . . . and now exhale, let it out . . . empty your tummy out, out, out. . . ." I search for air like I'm crawling to Aqaba for water. This is good; I'm centering myself and teaching them at the same time. I keep my eyes closed and continue.

"Pretend your tummy is a balloon and fill it up with air," I say. "Now let the air out, squeeze it out, out, out. . . ."

My arms are raised, and I blink my eyes open to check on their progress. Ten kids stare back at me, blank. Not one of them has their eyes closed, and none of them appear to be deep breathing. Or breathing at all, for that matter.

"What? Is there a problem? You don't understand . . . or what?"

They laugh outright at me. They kill themselves laughing. Falling over each other, laughing at me. They hit each other and begin to topple down the risers, all the while laughing and laughing. Screeching laughing.

Tap, tap, tap.

The knocking is louder this time. I run to the door and open it, and, again, no one is there. I step outside to see if anyone is even nearby. No one. *What the hell?*

I stride back and face the kids, ignoring their hysteria. My shoulders are pressed tight. I'm straight as an arrow. *Get a grip.*

"I figure every good club needs mottos, and I'm going to teach you ours." I hold up three fingers and recite:

1. WE HELP EACH OTHER.
2. WE SHARE WITH EACH OTHER.
3. WE HONOR THE WORKS OF WILLIAM SHAKESPEARE.

"All together with me." I hold up one, two, and finally three fingers, and they whisper the mottos along with me.

"Pretty good, but let's do that again and act like we mean it," I twinkle. "One, two, thr—"

"WE HELP EACH OTHER! WE SHARE WITH EACH OTHER! WE HONOR THE WORKS OF WILLIAM SHAKESPEARE!"

I stagger back from their thunder. "Okay, that was better."

In that moment, I think these mottos may be no more than an adult's fantasy. Helping and sharing with each other? Most of these kids are eight, nine, and ten. At this age, the gaps between them are as wide as the Grand Canyon.

Tap, tap, tap. Good God, again with the door.

"Gosh, I'm so sorry, guys, hang on." I dash to the door, fling it open . . . no one. Back and forth, I scurry like an insane juggler in a circus.

"Um . . . Miss . . . umm . . ." A large, dark-haired girl jammed into a corner in the back row throws her arm high.

"Mel, you can just call me Mel. What's your name?"

"*I'm* Dana."

"Oh, okay. Dana. What's up?"

"It's the little kids. The little kids are banging on the wall when you're not looking. You think it's the door, but it's them." She slouches back against the wall.

I drill a look into the door. The door is no longer my friend. Instead, it's the culprit. I'm slammed with the kids' howls, which pierce me like shards of ice. I blush crimson, and the sweat starts to flow.

When I'd proposed this program to the principal, she asked how much it would cost.

"No charge," I'd answered. I figured that if they paid me, I'd be hired, and if I was hired, I'd be stuck, and I didn't want to be stuck. As a volunteer, they couldn't fire me, and I could quit if the whole thing went south.

I'm as hot now as if I were sunbathing in the Caribbean. My head is aching. I can't get my thoughts in order. Where's that escape hatch I had so carefully planned? *Damn, dammit to hell anyway.* Where's their gratitude? My cheerful disposition has vanished, and I want to run. I want to run out that bloody door and across the cement playground. I want to run up the 405 Freeway and up the 5 Freeway and go back to Canada, a country I haven't lived in for over twenty years, but maybe it would welcome me home. Oh God, I want to run.

Dana, my informant, is a twelve-year-old in fifth grade. She's a big-boned girl, a Gulliver surrounded by cute, small kids. What is she doing here? What am I doing here? We don't belong.

Tap, tap, tap. My grandma's stubby fingers anchored a nail, and she hammered it into a dusty plank. *Tap, tap, tap.* Our Grandma was a stocky, determined powerhouse. My brothers and I watched her work on a warm summer morning.

Mom and Dad, away for a week, had Grandma travel west from the prairies to look after us.

On this day, she created a project. Grandma discovered a pile of old wooden boards in a back corner of the yard, hauled them out one by one, and set them on the weed-laden dirt. She dragged two additional long beams to lay perpendicular to the first lot. She found Dad's hammer and a coffee tin of rusty nails.

I was eight. My brothers were six and four. Mystified, we cocked our heads.

Grandma frowned, pounded the nails, checked her palms for splinters, and wiped sweat from her brow. Periodically, she stood back to survey the progress. She used the apron tied around her plump waist to clean her clammy hands and made an adjustment by kicking a plank back in line.

When she was done, Grandma upturned two empty white buckets and instructed my brothers to sit. She handed them each a small bowl of popcorn and a cup of contraband tea. Grandma let us have tea, which was normally reserved for adults, once she'd doctored it with hot milk and two teaspoons of sugar. She scraped a kitchen chair across the dirt yard and plopped down next to my brothers. They wolfed down their treats, she gave me a nod, and I knew what I must do.

Up I stepped, shyly nudging the toe of my thin-soled sneaker onto the wood. From above, sunbeams ricocheted off the lenses of my glasses. I clamped my hands on bony hips and forced my elbows to point east and west. Grandma and my brothers watched and waited.

I was onstage. Grandma had built me a stage, and here I was in front of a real audience.

I pretended to tap dance with clumsy improvised steps. I twirled like a ballerina I'd seen on TV. My skinny legs dripped out of worn cotton shorts instead of a fluffy tutu. I sang "The Teddy Bear's Picnic," "Catch a Falling Star," and "Sugar Shack." My confidence grew, and I took languorous sweeping bows at the end of each number. Grandma ribbed the boys to clap. When they started twitching, she fed them more popcorn.

This was one of the best days of my childhood. Not because she had given me a theater but because Grandma knew who I was before I even had a clue.

When my parents returned home, the wood was torn apart. My stern-faced mom yanked each nail out and dropped them clanging back into the coffee can.

"But Mom—"

"People will think we're nuts. This is ridiculous." She dragged the lumber back to the corner of the yard.

Unwittingly, I'd been caught in the crosshairs of a lifelong fight between my mother and her mother. Every summer, Mom would pack us onto a train to visit her family essentially to duke it out with Grandma. At the end of a week's visit, we raced to the train station to get home, my head reeling with the creepy images of tear-stained adult cheeks after their bloodcurdling battles.

After Grandma left that summer, I stood on tiptoe on my single bed and peeped over the windowsill in the dark of night. The two abandoned buckets shone white in the moonlight.

"The audience," I whispered.

My grandma saw, and she knew: I was nothin' without an audience. *Tap, tap, tap.*

Tap, tap, tap. I wait a second and eye the group. I will catch you, imp. *Bang, bang, bang.* It's so loud that we all turn to the demanding door. *Bang, bang, bang.*

I lope to the entrance and open it to Grace and Carla. I'm never going to get this right. They saunter past me, and I sneak a look at my watch. How much longer, oh Lord, *how much longer?*

I balance the atlas on my knees, tilt it outward, and direct the kids' attention to England. Peering over the book's top, I point out where William Shakespeare lived in Stratford-upon-Avon and where he traveled to London to begin his career. Because I'm busy running my finger over roads and rivers and not watching *them*, I miss the real action going on in the room.

Kick, push, shove, hit. Cushions fly at me from the top of the risers, and Marin stares me down. She's tightly wired and crammed between the group's two boys, Miles and Daniel. She elbows each boy, one after the other. *Dig right, jab left.* She keeps her gaze glued to mine as she does this.

"Who threw these?" I hold up two pillows, bypassing Marin's challenge.

A cacophony of blame comes at me.

"She—"

"No, *he*—"

"No, *they*—"

"Okay!" I shout. "Fine. Forget it and stop it. Don't throw stuff. That's disrespectful. We're borrowing this library for today, and we want to leave it nice . . . right?" I sound so pathetic, like those lame teachers everyone remembers and snickers about.

Marin kicks Daniel. The heel of her shoe digs into his thigh. The boy yelps as if stabbed.

"What are you doing?"

I stand. Marin's reply is a shrug.

I return to my chair and retrieve the atlas. "When we look at where Stratford-upon-Avon is, it seems close to London, but it took William Shakespeare a long—"

Tap, tap, tap. For God's sake. I snap my head, and Daniel grins. I wasn't quick enough to catch him rapping on the wall. I hate him. The rage is instant. It rips up my back and blazes through my eyes.

What am I saying? He's a *third grader.* That reaction just bought me a dandy condo in hell.

Miles squints and sizes me up. Whenever I look at him, he's checking me out. I give him a small smile and hope for a like response. It doesn't come.

"Can I get some water?" Daniel asks, already on the move.

"Uh . . . yeah, sure—" The door slams before I can finish.

"Can I go to the bathroom?"

"Me too, I really have to go."

The door is repeatedly banged shut as they run off and leave me nodding like a bobblehead doll.

Every actor knows what it's like to bomb onstage. For the first time in my life, I can't hold my audience. These kids are bored and fidgety. They don't want to sit still and learn. I'm desperate. What to do when you're flopping big time? I stretch my arms overhead, blow air from my lips, scratch my head, and beg the ceiling for an answer.

And I spot him. He winks at me and gives me an idea. Captain Underpants to the rescue. I look at the kids.

"Four hundred years ago, not only were there no video games, there were also no bathrooms in the houses. The Elizabethans used buckets and threw their poo and pee out their windows."

This piece of information garners cries of "Eeeew!" and "Gross!"

I proceed with worse.

"People walking down below on the street had to duck and run, or they'd get hit with that awful stuff. The citizens held handkerchiefs over their noses. These were filled with lavender and rosemary and were called nosegays. They needed them because the smell was so horrible."

Not a sound.

Unchained like a wayward locomotive, I use the word *poop* in almost every sentence.

"Ladies had dried mud and old poop stuck to the edges of their beautiful long dresses."

I have them.

"Dog poop, horse poop, and people poop all mixed together. These folks couldn't wait for a good rainfall to clean things up."

"Eeeew!"

"Yeeech!"

They cover their own noses as if they can smell poop in the library.

They're with me. I speak faster.

"So, Elizabeth I was Queen of England. That's why we call this time the Elizabethan period."

Regina's face is solemn as she absorbs this.

"Elizabeth was the daughter of King Henry VIII. Oh, that King Henry was quite a guy. He got married six times. A very fussy fellow, Henry VIII was."

I hold up a book with a picture of fat, old King Henry and a red-haired Queen Elizabeth.

"You see," I say, pointing to the queen, "she has very pale skin. That's the white makeup she plastered on to cover up spots after a bout with chickenpox."

They lean in close to see Elizabeth's face.

"Do you notice the white ruffle around her neck?"

They nod.

"I think that looks like an air filter from Pep Boys."

They nod again, very serious.

"Henry's favorite pastime was eating. That guy ate so much chicken and beef and so many pies that his helpers had to build him a special cart to wheel him around the castle."

They share giggles over tubby King Henry.

"Henry was married to Elizabeth's mother, Anne Boleyn, but because she had a girl baby and not a boy baby, he had Anne Boleyn's head cut right off."

In the theatre, we call this "whoring your audience." Cheap, cheap, cheap . . . but nary a peep. Guilty as charged.

"Kings were very powerful. You were never allowed to look a king straight in the eye. You had to kneel in his presence, and the king could decide if he wanted to take your land, your children, or your farm animals. People were either very rich or very poor during this time."

"Excuse me, um . . . Miss . . . um—"

"Mel, you can just call me Mel."

Regina places her hands together as if praying.

"What if I said . . . "

She widens her eyes and tips her chin skyward. She adopts an English accent from some other incarnation. ". . . please, *please* sir, please Your Highness, could I have just a little bit of food?"

Here's a Juliet if I ever saw one.

"Off with your head!" I yell.

They scream. Thank God, the first laugh that's *with* me, not *at* me. I launch back in with more ghastly information.

"Another problem for the Elizabethans was the Black Plague, a disease so contagious that millions of people died of it. If someone in your family caught the plague, your house was boarded and locked up with all of you in it. Your dad had to lower a basket out of a window to the ground and hope that the neighbors would put food into it to keep your family alive. No one was allowed out until you had a clean bill of health."

"Was there El Pollo Loco?"

"No, Miles, there was no El Pollo Loco." I make a sad face. "Really, there wasn't much to look forward to in those difficult days. Except—"

I pause with my index finger lifted skyward in a dramatic gesture.

"—going to the theater. You and I like to go to the movies, and the Elizabethans loved going to the theater for fun."

I sneak a peek at the clock. Time has whipped by. I'm exceedingly grateful.

"Look, here's what I have for you." I hold up a bright blue notebook.

"We get those?" Stella shouts. "Our very own?"

Stella is a stocky eight-year-old in third grade. She's loud and in-your-face. She guffaws like Aunt Gertie at a Christmas party.

"Of course, there's one for each of you, and look what else." I hold up the packets of colored pens. They squeal. I'm practically ready to pull out a wad of cash, I'm so relieved they don't hate me. "Please put your name on the front of your journal and write or draw something you learned today."

They speed off to corners in the library with their notebooks and pens and pencils. They hide under tables and desks. I'm wondering about this protocol when Dana asks, "Can I write 'Dear Kitty' in my journal?" She's remained tucked into a corner at the top of the risers.

"Sure, that would be fine."

Dear Kitty. *Dear Kitty?* It rings a bell: *The Diary of Anne Frank.* This girl reads. And writes.

Exhausted, I drop into my chair, rest my chin in my hand, and study them as they write or draw or throw pencils at each other.

Who are these people, these children, these terrors? I think this is a mistake. I plan a speech for the principal. I'll take the blame, chalk it up to inexperience, and apologize for my grandiosity. I can't run a Shakespeare program with my primary tool being the word *poop*.

"Hey, is this over?" Daniel demands, snapping me from my reverie.

"Yeah. Yeah, it's over. You can go, Daniel."

And he does. Fast. He grabs a backpack and speeds away. The other kids take Daniel's lead and follow suit, yelling and elbowing each other to get out the door.

Dana pauses on her way past me. "Thanks, Miss . . . um . . . thanks for doing this," she stammers.

"Oh, sure, you're welcome. Bye." I peel myself up to gather errant pens and pencils and clean up the mess left behind. I'm tossing paper into the trash when the door opens behind me. It's Stella. Guess she forgot something.

"See you next week!" she yells.

There she is, standing in the doorway, with a huge grin on her face.

"Yeah," I whisper.

And with a tinny clang, the escape hatch slams shut.

Off with my head.

CHILDREN'S WRITES

Dear Diares,
I read that London had a fat king. They have a qeen in London. The prun peolep have no food. The rich peolpe have lots for food. They no the bath room in the house. They roon the pooh in the sreet.

LESSON PLAN

Teachers know this axiom: *never let them go in groups.* Going to the bathroom and getting water are "Get Out of Jail Free" cards.

My husband, William, glances up as I drag my ass through the front door.

"A large goblet of wine, my liege," I say as I drop my purse and stumble to a chair.

"How'd it go?" he asks, pouring the burgundy.

"They think I'm four hundred years old."

"Did you tell them you're only two hundred?"

"Remind me again why I want to do this?"

"I have no idea why you want to do this. Want a bath?"

"Yes, please." He goes to fill the tub. I take a big slug and refill my glass.

Months before, a flyer had been dropped on our porch. It was a plea for help from a group of neighborhood parents wishing to make Arden Street Elementary the best school possible. The school had a dedicated principal and teaching staff, but these days, civilian help was the key to success in public schools. I attended a booster club meeting of five parents, one neighbor volunteer, and the principal. The principal wanted to make Arden Street a "neighborhood school."

Every morning, seven yellow school buses pulled up in front of the school, and children poured out. Every afternoon, the same buses were reloaded with these students and drove them back to destinations up to twenty miles across the city because their nearby campuses had either closed or were at capacity. A "neighborhood school," I was told, would mean more parents would be involved because they would be local.

When I researched local school statistics, I learned a couple of things. First, Arden Street Elementary was a Title I school, meaning the government gave it extra money because most of its kids came from low-income families. Also, Arden Street was 95 percent non-white, while at other schools in our area, the demographics were near reversed.

The twelve kids who showed up for Shakespeare Club reflected these numbers. Eleven of them came from Spanish-speaking households. Their parents or grandparents had traveled far to get them here. Daniel was our lone African-American member. We had only two Caucasian representatives: me and that giant icon of Anglo-Saxon literature, William Shakespeare.

This was the state of the school that was asking for help at a time when I was lost and empty of purpose.

The first thing I did was to take a one-day training course to become a reading mentor. I was paired up to read once a week with a first grader named Charley.

I loved being with Charley to explore the realms of Dr. Seuss and Clifford the Big Red Dog. Flush with the fulfillment of helping Charley learn to read, I had blurted out to the principal my idea for starting the Shakespeare Club.

I sink into the scalding bath, dip down to my mouth, and blow bubbles of soapy water. What made me think that individual sessions with a six-year-old could compare to what I had attempted today?

Tears well. I rub my fingers over my eyes, and the sobs percolate. *I can't do this.*

I thought, hoped, and wished I could, but I couldn't. I love the theatre and miss the theatre, but this idea of replacing my dreams and dumping them on these children is so stupid that I can't stand it. I'm in a black hole.

I wipe my face with a washcloth and scrub it, searching for some raw truth.

A wise woman once suggested to me that, when in such a dark place, it is perhaps a waste of energy to fight your way out. Sometimes the trick is to sit quietly, accept the dimness, and wait until your eyes adjust.

CHAPTER II

MY KINGDOM FOR A FLUTE

> If it be now, 'tis not to come; if it be not to come,
> it will be now; if it be not now, yet it will come—
> the readiness is all.
>
> *Hamlet* Act V, Scene II

It's pretty clear that Hamlet is on the verge of a nervous breakdown when it comes to taking action. Filled with self-loathing and despair, he doesn't know what to do or when to do it or how to do it.

I get Hamlet.

But do I need a whistle?

"We have lots and lots of whistles," says Elena, a school secretary. She pulls out a box filled with silver whistles. "Lots of teachers use whistles. It's okay to use one," she reassures me.

I nod and consider the prospect of a chrome whistle dangling around my neck. I don't want to be a gym teacher or a prison warden.

"Thanks, Elena, but as crazy as this sounds, I'm going to try and control the situation, somehow, without a whistle."

Elena shakes her head as she tucks the whistle box away. No doubt she's seen it all. A fool and her whistle are soon parted.

The Shakespeare Club has moved out of the library and into our permanent home of Room 15. There's a whiteboard across the front wall, and in the center of the room is a rug imprinted with a map of the United States. I amble over the carpet, stepping on state after colorful state. Orange for California, red for

Arizona. I wish I were on a road trip.

I'd pull into a town in Texas and order up a longneck and some barbecue. I'd study the locals from my spot at a wooden bar, clicking the heels of my new cowboy boots on the rungs of the stool. I'd imagine living there in a small cottage with a garden and a cat. Those strangers would be my friends. After my beer and ribs, I'd check into a roadside motel with a flashing neon sign that cried VACANCY. I'd tuck in under thin polyester sheets with a good book. Anonymous. Alone. Away. I like road trips.

But I'm not in Abilene. It's a balmy fall afternoon, and I'm alone in Room 15 of Arden Street Elementary. I open my Shakespeare Club box filled with notebooks, Scotch tape, scissors, and string. I don't know why I packed string. Be prepared, I guess.

On tables scattered about the room, I lay down the kids' journals, one after another, making sure they're straight and evenly spaced. Beside each notebook, I place a freshly sharpened pencil. I hum as I do this because I like setting tables. I like arranging flowers and polishing wine glasses, choosing music and lighting candles. I've done my homework, and I'm here today full of fresh energy.

There are lots of teaching sites online with tips on classroom management. One consistent admonition from the pros is organization. Be ready with a tight schedule in order to run a tight ship.

I set library books along the whiteboard ledge. I hope to inspire them in their journal work with the drawings of Elizabeth I, the photos of Stratford, and the colorful sketches of Elizabethan life. I arrange twelve chairs in a horseshoe. I place mine to face them and sit. After a few seconds, I push my chair a little further back. It needs to be perfect so that I can see all of them and they can see me as the captain. The empty chairs stare at me as I rehearse how this will go.

"Hello! Hi! Hey there!" *Hmmmm . . .* warming up my vocal cords. "Hey guys!"

I'll smile and welcome them as they arrive. I'll be the gracious hostess. "How was your day?" I'll ask in a warm voice. "Can I take your backpack? Please, take a seat. Your hair looks lovely today, Stella. Well, I'm delighted to see you, too, Daniel."

Deep breath, exhale, drop the shoulders. I'm serene and confident.

The school bell shatters the peace with a loud peal. Fear courses like an electric current through my arms, and my deep breaths become shallow gasps. I could be in a dark alley at midnight. I'm out of my seat, whipping my head to the open door. They're outside. I can hear them laughing and chattering. I consider hiding and then—

Here they come tumbling into Room 15 in a jumble, one on top of another until we're face to face and I don't know what to say.

What's my line? What do I do? What's my character?

They fling backpacks of vibrant pinks, blues, and yellows to the floor, creating a small mountain. They dive for their seats, fighting each other for position. Chairs are tipped over, the kids' small bodies crash over the United States carpet, and their voices clamor louder and louder.

"Do not move the chairs. *Do not move the chairs!*" I don't remember rehearsing that line. In fact, I distinctly recall telling myself *there will be no need to raise your voice ever.*

Not that they notice my shrieking. There's only one thing to do in a situation like this: shout louder.

"Do NOT move the chairs! STOP!"

Freeze frame. All eyes are on me. Stella is horizontal across three chairs, her head propped in her palm as if she were reclining on a couch. Other children are caught in mid-crawl, on their backs, or on top of other children.

The clock on the wall mocks me with 2:45 p.m.; I have an hour and fifteen minutes to go. What I don't have are twelve children, hands folded and ready for my stellar stories of Elizabethan England and William Shakespeare.

There's a rustle behind me. I spin around and catch the eye of a woman standing in the doorway. Busted. She's going to hand me over to the school authorities. Her arm is around the shoulders of a young girl. The woman waves at me with a smile. She's friendly, and I like her immediately. She reaches a hand out to me, and we shake gently.

"I'm Tina," she says. "I teach third grade."

"Oh, hi." I turn my back to the room, lean against the doorframe, and pretend this teacher and I are simply colleagues enjoying a chat. The kids are probably hanging from the lights and perching on cabinets behind me, but I ignore their commotion.

Fortunately, Tina's polite and doesn't mention the racket. How kind she is. I would like to buy her something.

"This is Azra." Tina looks at her charge. "She's in my class and would like to join Shakespeare Club. Her mommy didn't know it started last week, so we hope it isn't too late."

I kneel down to Azra. Her eyes are large and blue, surrounded by dark, long lashes, so long that they brush against the lenses of her eyeglasses. Azra is Muslim and wears a *hijab*, or headscarf.

"Hi, Azra, welcome to the Shakespeare Club."

"Thank you," Tina says. "Bye!" And she vaporizes before I can beg her to stay and teach me how to teach.

Azra shoots me a shy smile and sits in a chair I've added to the horseshoe. Grace and Carla race to join Azra, sitting on either side of her and holding her hands as if they own her.

"We told Azra to come to Shakespeare Club, and we told her she would like it," Carla informs me.

"I certainly hope she does. Good recruiting, by the way."

Carla beams, even if she's not entirely sure what I mean. The noise in the room escalates. I have to locate my calm voice and poise. My throat already stings a little from the strain of yelling.

"Okay, my little friends, you will reset the chairs and you will sit in the chairs, one to a person, so we can begin."

Surprisingly, they do. They regroup and wait upright. A quick head count reveals twelve bodies, but only one boy, Daniel. One empty chair blinks at me. *Where's Miles?* I begin roll call.

"Um, Miss . . . ah . . . um . . ."

"Mel, you can call me Mel."

On the board is MEL RYANE, circled. "There you go, that's my name. Yes . . ." I check my list. "Candace?"

"Jordanna."

"Oh, right, sorry, Jordanna."

"I'm Candace," says Candace, which is complicated, because she is a replica of Jordanna.

Exactly what I need, identical twins. Here lies the road to madness. Both girls are dressed in matching blue and white satin athletic jackets with BABY GIRL printed across the front.

"Okay, yes. Jordanna?"

"You can call me Jordan."

"You got it, Jordan." *Prefers to be called Jordan.* I don't know how to break it to her that I will likely be calling her Jordan *and* Candace because I can't imagine getting it straight. Both girls have long brown hair that's parted in the middle and soft brown eyes.

"What's up?" I ask

"Miles is hiding." Jordan jerks her head to a corner of the room behind a dividing wall.

"Thanks." I tiptoe for a look.

"Miles. Miles," I call. I discover him crammed into an alcove. His legs are scrunched up with his feet curled against a stack of boxes. His face, turned sideways, rests on his knees, and he giggles.

"Hey there, what's going on? Are you going to join us?"

Miles's laughter escalates because it's fun to hide from the teacher and then make her find you.

"Come on, Miles, let's go." I move away, hoping he'll follow. And he does. He crawls out of his foxhole and slides into the empty chair.

Meanwhile, the gang has once again collapsed. They out-yell each other and laugh and laugh. I wait and wait until I realize I could end up waiting forever. They're fine. They're having a good old time. They don't notice me. They can't take a hint.

"Eyes closed," I launch. "All of them, all two eyes in your head, closed. Picture your belly button, inhale deeply, expand your tummy like a balloon and hold the breath . . . one . . . two . . . three . . . " I wave my hand over peeping eyes. "CLOSED . . . four . . . five . . . six . . . and exhale . . . "

Marin is staring at me. Eyes wide as moons, she studies me like a cop. I move to her and gently put a finger on her forehead, nod, and whisper, "Eyes closed."

Her eyes remain open.

"Okay, next . . . Child's Pose," I say with a lilt.

"Whaaaaat?" they mock.

"Child's Pose. It's yoga. If you want to be cool, you really should know yoga, and I'm going to teach you. It's an excellent way to get calm and centered before acting."

I once saw a news program about an entire school that started each day with meditation and yoga. The results were impressive: children were attentive in class, scored high on exams, and expressed themselves creatively. This was also my plan, and one day, the Governor of California (the state in orange) will give me a medal, and children will cheer me in gratitude for changing their lives.

I kneel, rest my forehead on the floor, and stretch my arms across the carpet. "See? Easy and it feels so good. You try it."

They throw themselves on the floor, but they don't copy me. They roll on their backs and their stomachs. They spin across the carpet and crash into each other.

"Eeew, it stinks!"

"Someone farted!"

"Yeeech!"

"Farty farty!"

Screams of laughter.

"Alright, no talking to your neighbor and no looking around. You start by kneeling, then drop your bottom—" I say, attempting to regain control.

"Bottom!" they scream. "Bottoms are where farts come from!"

"Yeeech!"

"Bottom, bottom, bottom!"

They love that word, *bottom*, and I have a sinking feeling. The play I've chosen for them, *A Midsummer Night's Dream*, just happens to have a central character named Bottom.

Then the kicking starts, followed by the shoving and the pushing. My forehead is on the carpet as I rest in a perfect Child's Pose. I could use a whistle right about now. I unravel myself up off the floor and shout, "Order! Order! I call this meeting to order!"

There is no order. I clap my hands and attempt to herd them to their seats. Miles has disappeared again. I consider going on another hunt but think better of it. If he wants to live inside a shelving unit, let him. I may join him.

Eventually. I have something resembling order. I hold up a sheaf of papers. "This is called 'The Pied Piper.'"

The cover page has a sketch of the Piper playing his pipe with a drove of rats following him. Robert Browning penned the poem in 1888, so its language was archaic, but I expected that a tale of disappearing rats and children would hold their interest.

"This is about a town filled with rats and people very afraid of getting the plague. Sit quietly and I'll read."

They're remarkably silent as I begin:

> *Hamelin Town's in Brunswick,*
> *By famous Hanover City,*
> *The river Weser deep and wide,*
> *Washes its wall on the southern side,*

A pleasanter spot you never spied,
But, when begins my ditty,
Almost five hundred years ago,
To see the townsfolk suffer so
From vermin was a pity.

Within seconds, I realize I've made an entirely stupid choice. The kids' faces register an astonished array of squints, frowns, and utter disgust. Jaws hang aghast that I actually thought this would be entertaining.

I can hardly blame them. Whoever heard of Hamelin and a river named Weser and who in the real world uses words like *ditty*? With the Pied Piper papers in my hand, I'm in trouble. This had been my big plan for today's session.

When actors find themselves working with a loquacious director, they often want to scream, "Just tell me: louder/softer/faster/slower." In this instance, I choose *faster* and attempt to race through Browning's story in a single, sustained breath. I cut out whole chunks like a desperate salesman faced with a thinning audience.

The mayor sent East, West, North and South,
To offer the Piper, by word of mouth,
Wherever it was men's lots to find him,
Silver and gold to his heart's content. . . .

I blaze through the text as fast as those rats following the Piper until, at the brink of the old river Weser, I stop. I'm out of air. Silence.

"Remember the Black Death? We talked about it last week? Schools, churches, and theaters had to be closed down because if people gathered in large groups, the illness could easily spread? Remember that?" I ask.

"What did they do?" Regina whispers, serious. "What did they do if they couldn't go to those places?"

"Well, they stayed at home and read books or played cards or board games. You know, kind of like when we get rainstorms and you can't play outside?"

"Yeah, no school." Daniel nods. "Sweet."

"How do you think it would feel if you were the Pied Piper and you did your part by getting rid of the rats, but the mayor and townspeople decided they didn't want to pay you?"

"No fair!" they shout in a chorus.

"Then you might want revenge, right?"

Blank looks.

"You know, like when someone does something to you that isn't fair or nice? Maybe when someone says you did something bad and you really didn't?"

They remember past crimes and dart looks to one another.

"That's when we want revenge. We want that person to feel as bad as we do, and so it was with the Pied Piper."

Miles, reemerged from his shelter, is half-listening at the room's edge as he picks his way through a basket of counting blocks. As I speak to the group, I sidle up to him, remove the toys from his hands, and lead him back to his chair. He sits dramatically, as if facing electrocution.

"The Pied Piper got his revenge. He took away all the children by playing his pipe in a magical way. All those kids skipped, danced, and followed him over hill and dale—all but one, a little lame boy who couldn't keep up and now was the only child left in Hamelin." I hold up a page with the little lame boy, balancing on one feeble crutch, all alone in the town square. "Then the grown-ups were very sad because they missed their children, but that was the price they paid for not keeping their end of the bargain by refusing to pay the Pied Piper the one thousand guilders they'd promised."

"One thousand," Daniel whispers. "Sweet."

"Where did they go?" a girl named Jennifer asks.

"Rumor has it that they went off to a wonderful land with golden streets and clowns and cotton candy and all the rides you could imagine."

"For free?" Daniel asks.

"Absolutely, all for free."

"Sweet."

"But here's the thing: imagine you were the Pied Piper, and after a busy day of eating hot dogs and riding roller coasters, you had to tuck these children into little beds, and you started to hear sniffles."

"They're crying." Anna, a fifth grader with braces on her teeth, is wearing a fluffy pink boa wound twice around her neck and trailing down her skinny arms.

"Yes, Anna, they're crying because they miss their real beds and they miss their moms and dads. So, for a while, the Pied Piper was happy because he had his revenge, but look at what he's left with."

I let this sink in.

"He now has to take care of lots and lots of unhappy children."

Robert Browning is cursing me from the great beyond as I fabricate a new ending to his story.

"William Shakespeare wrote many plays about revenge, and we'll see what happens when characters seek payback. What do you think? Is that cool or what?"

"Sweet."

Thanks, Daniel.

"Marin, what do you think of this story?"

"Kinda boring." She shrugs.

"Jennifer?"

"Mmmm, not so great."

Jennifer is a pretty girl, but she doesn't carry herself like she knows it. She lacks that "look at me" swagger. She doesn't flip her hair or focus on her clothes, adjusting and readjusting like the pretty girls do. I wasn't a pretty girl or didn't think I was . . . or didn't know.

At the age of eleven, dressed in a stiff, homemade, navy blue uniform, I was sent off to Girl Guide Camp in the woods of Canada. My mother insisted that black Oxford shoes would last longer than the trendy sneakers everyone else was wearing, and I was relegated to the status of outsider. My footwear matched my brown-framed, thick-lensed eyeglasses. Spending time alone was familiar to me.

At camp, I liked the singing 'round the campfire stuff and hiking through sun-dappled trails, but you could keep those morning swim classes in an ice-cold lake. To escape those dips, I concocted a lie about an earache and was directed to spend swim hour in an empty cabin that housed exactly one book, abandoned on a cobwebbed windowsill.

It was a worn paperback copy of William Shakespeare's *Romeo and Juliet*. Its dry pages fluttered open in my hands. I whispered the poetry aloud and managed to follow the story, if not Shakespeare's vocabulary. I convinced myself I was Juliet. My clunky black shoes became silk slippers, my glasses fell away to reveal big blue eyes, and I tripped through a castle in an emerald-green velvet dress.

Dana's hand is raised. "Excuse me, are we doing a play?"

"Yes, *A Midsummer Night's Dream*. We start in January."

"For the whole school?" Jennifer starts to panic.

"I have no idea if it'll be for anybody yet. I think we should start work on it, take a vote, and decide if we want people to see it."

"Is there kissing?" Daniel shouts.

"Tons of kissing."

This entirely freaks them out.

"No, no!" Regina cries. "We're just kids! There's no kissing allowed, no kissing until you're twenty-one or thirty-nine!"

"I didn't know that rule. Glad you told me."

"Seriously, are you for real? Kissing?" Daniel's on a bender.

"Okay, I'm going to tell you the truth, but you must be quiet and listen."

They settle down, a little bit.

"When William Shakespeare wrote his plays, girls were not allowed to act. There was no such person as an actress. Only boys were allowed to act."

Shouts of triumph from Daniel and Miles.

"So, there was rarely kissing in his plays because boy actors were dressed like girls, and the audience didn't care to see boys kissing boys onstage, even if they looked like girls."

Gagging noises from the boys.

"That'll do, fellas. You may have heard of one of Shakespeare's more famous plays, *Romeo and Juliet*?"

"Yes, yes!" Dana bounces out of her seat. "I saw that movie with Leo— Leonardo . . . "

"That's correct, Leonardo DiCaprio played Romeo in a movie of the play. Romeo and Juliet meet in secret at night. She's up on her balcony, and he's on the ground. He has to jump the fence to get into her yard. Shakespeare wrote this very romantic scene that takes place with Juliet *upstairs* and Romeo *downstairs* so they couldn't actually kiss."

"Let's never do that play," Marin says. "Too much love stuff."

"Well, we won't do that play, but we will do a play with love stuff, so you might want to get your head around that."

Big *yeeech* sounds and more vomiting motions with fingers down throats.

I sneak a look at the clock and am thrilled to see it's time for journal writing.

"I've placed your journals where I'd like you to sit at the tables, so let's get to it."

"Nooooo, I don't waaaaannnt to sit there, nooooo, pleeeeeaaase!" Stella's shrieks pierce my head like cat claws on sheet metal.

"Stella, Stella, please don't tell me you're a whiner."

"Nooooo, buuuttttt—"

"Oh my gosh, you are. You're a whiner." I cover my ears and widen my eyes in shock.

"Pleeeeeaaassse—"

I put my hands on her shoulders. "Here's the deal, Stella. If you whine, you will get nothing you ask of me, ever. That's the way it will always be. It is unbecoming conduct. If you whine, you'll lose all your friends and never be asked to people's houses."

Stunned silence for a second, then: "But I don't waaaaannnt to sit theeeeer-rre. . . ."

I shrug and walk away. "Like I said."

Stella reluctantly agrees to sit in her appointed place, but I can hear her whisper-whining to Grace.

"Shhh!" I hiss, passing behind her. We've been together two weeks, and these kids have already formed cliques.

Journal writing time passes.

"So, here's the thing." My voice rises above the babble. "We won't be meeting next Thursday."

I'm surprised to get a chorus of "Why, why, why?"

"Don't you like us?" Jennifer asks.

"It's Thanksgiving, that's all. You get a school break. And when you get back from the holiday and turkey and fooling around, we'll meet then."

"No school!" Daniel yells. "Sweet!"

"Okay, then, happy Thanksgiving! Have a swell holiday and see ya later!"

And they're off, scrambling for backpacks and out the door. I begin to address the detritus when I hear a small voice behind me.

"Could I help you? Could I help you clean up?" It's Azra, all alone with those bright blue eyes blinking at me through her round spectacles.

"That would be great." I smile at Azra, who's like the little lame boy in the town square. The only child Hamelin got to keep, and I want to keep her.

We gather up journals and pens and rearrange chairs and tables. I open Azra's notebook. In it, she's drawn the queen in a bright pink dress with a gigantic crown on her head.

"Do you like the story of Queen Elizabeth, Azra?"

"Yes. She's a queen. And she's beautiful."

Azra seems to equate being queen with being pretty. I don't want to spoil this by telling her this queen may not have been a real looker with her ill-advised makeup job.

"The people of England loved her, too. Against the advice of her helpers, Queen Elizabeth rode her horse into the countryside and visited people in little villages."

"Oh," Azra whispers. "I like her." And then she closes her journal, caressing the cover with her small hand.

Azra's mom arrives at the door and waits for her daughter. Azra runs to her. "I drew a picture of Queen Elizabeth, and she has red hair and rides a horse."

They walk off, and for a second, I feel I might be good at this because someone else thinks I am. We're a mere two weeks into Shakespeare Club, but it seems much longer. No doubt because I'm actually four hundred and forty years old and a little creaky, despite the cool yoga poses.

CHILDREN'S WRITES

Dear Diary,

My family lives in a small house it is easy getting the pleg because there is a lot of rats in the street. I wish I could be rich so I could be in a house with someone else to protect me from the black pleg. The Queen is lucky because she is pretty and she is protected by guards from people and things that could harm her.

LESSON PLAN

My sister-in-law teaches in an elementary school and told me, "Don't hope or wish or plan on being liked. It is simply not important that they like you."

No problem. That "Like me! Like me!" stuff is for suckers and sissies.

Yeah. Right.

As I sign out in the office's volunteer book, Elena looks at me from behind her desk. "Whistle?" she asks.

"Keep that box handy, but not just yet."

Next to me, a weepy third-grade teacher is filling out paperwork. I don't want to pry, but it might be too cold to ignore her.

"Are you okay?" I ask.

"It's the system." She shakes her head.

"What do you mean?"

"They keep pushing kids up and up when they aren't ready, when they can't even read, so they'll drop out down the line. These are the children who quit, and we wonder why the statistics are so high. . . . " Her voice trails off.

"Yeah." I don't know what to say.

Educational researchers call this epidemic "failing upward." The dropout rate in the United States is ridiculously high. In California, officials agree that somewhere between 40 and 50 percent of African-American and Latino high school students are not graduating. Classrooms are overstuffed, and teachers are doing their best to cram test answers into growing brains. Some days, it must seem hopeless.

Six-year-old Charley and I are still reading together. Lately, we have started *Curious George*. It has taken Charley weeks and weeks to read the word *curious*. I try games using the word.

"Charley, I am *curious*, what did you eat for breakfast?"

"Cereal."

"Charley, I am *curious*, what kind of cereal did you eat?"

"Cheerios."

"Charley, are you *curious* about me?"

Charley shakes his head.

"Nothing at all? You can ask anything you want."

Charley shakes his head.

I might be dull, but Curious George isn't, and we turn another page.

Charley starts a passage and collapses on the library table. His head lies atop his hands as he faces me. Why is reading so tiring for Charley?

I have the school nurse check his eyesight. She says it's fine. I do little tests for dyslexia, but he is A-okay with that, too. Reading is just a huge effort for Charley.

Charley loves watching wrestling on television with his dad and brothers.

He has brought me a picture of a *lucha libre* mask. On the playground, Charley chases soccer balls and bashes tetherballs. Charley is bilingual. His parents attend all the school functions Charley participates in, but they can't sit on the couch and read with him.

On days Charley and I read in the library, we'll sometimes run into Shakespeare Club members.

"Look!" Stella says, grabbing my attention with a book on Queen Elizabeth I.

"See?" Grace says, holding up a copy of *Hamlet*.

Wow, they're searching for books on the Elizabethan period and works by or about William Shakespeare.

"Gosh, girls, I'm impressed you're finding these books, but you have to leave Charley and me alone now. We're reading about a little curious monkey."

Chapter III

EVERYONE HAS A PRICE

It is a good divine that follows his own instructions;
I can easier teach twenty
what were good to be done,
than to be one of the twenty to follow mine own teaching.
The Merchant of Venice Act I, Scene II

What can I do better? What can I say to them? How can I make Elizabe-thans as fun as Nanny McPhee?

Why don't they remember my name?

It's the middle of the night, and thoughts are pinging around my head. I bolt upright, spilling the cat to the floor and sending William rolling to the other side of the bed.

They can't call me Mel. They can't, and they won't. They don't call adults by their first names.

So, when I get to Room 15, I write on the board: MS. RYANE.

I stand back, erase it, and print it bigger, clearer, and then circle it. Today, I'm wearing a chocolate brown sweater set and beige corduroys. I've taken time with my makeup before getting to school. I rarely put mascara on to impress William, but I dress for success for eight-year-olds.

Look good, feel good, do good. *Breathe.*

"Just promise them something," a first-grade teacher has told me. "Then they'll behave. I tell them they can see a movie or play a game, but they have to earn it with good behavior."

"So, bribery?"

"It works."

I'd typed out an agenda with bullet points of what to do during the ninety minutes I have with the kids.

- roll call
- deep breathing
- club mottos
- Child's Pose
- new rules
- the story of William Shakespeare

I look over the list, trying to memorize it, and tuck it away under my binder. Handy enough for referral, but if they catch a peek, I'm dead. One glance at my itinerary could result in one kid having insider knowledge over the others, and gloating would ensue.

I play a CD of ambient forest sounds. Chirping birds and hooting owls will instill a sense of calm in all of us. I go over my bribery plan as the sound of gentle wind pours from the CD player, hushing me into a sense of leadership. Iron fist in a velvet glove.

And in they come, tossing backpacks, screaming and jostling each other. They munch away on Crunchy Flamin' Hot Cheetos, the prepubescent snack food of choice. They smear bright cheese-colored fingerprints everywhere and grind errant morsels into the carpet. California is no longer the only orange state.

"What's this?" Stella sneers upon hearing woodland critters chirping from the boom box.

"The soothing sounds of the forest," I purr. "Can you hear the birds and the wind?"

"Oooh, yeeech—"

"Don't start with that, Stella."

She grins and grabs more Cheetos from Carla. Across the room, Marin lifts the corner of my binder and peers at my notes. I scoot over.

"Whatcha doin'?"

"Nothing." She springs back and smiles with cool detachment.

"Good," I say, but I keep my eye on her as she moves to whisper in Jennifer's ear.

Dana sidles over to catch the scoop. Three girls in a confab, and I kick myself for not burying those notes even deeper.

"Ms. Ryane." I point to my name on the board. "I know this is how you address adults, and that is as it should be. So, Ms. Ryane is my name. Feel free to use it."

And they do. At a higher decibel than I would like, but it soars out of their mouths.

"Ms. Ryane!"

"*Ms. Ryane!*"

"MS. RYANE!"

"Criminy, don't wear it out."

"When we do the play? Will we wear costumes?" Stella, of course.

"Who's coming?" Carla shouts.

"Is the whole school coming?" Jordan grimaces.

"I can't do that in front of the school. They'll laugh at us!" Candace tops her sister.

"Not my cousins, *please* don't let my cousins come! Ms. Ryane, promise no cousins!" Jennifer is frantic, and I'm puzzled since she's currently in the room with two of her cousins, Stella and Miles. Perhaps there is an additional assemblage of Jennifer cousins, and they all happen to be theatre critics. I choose to let this discussion take a backseat to the escalating panic.

You'd think I was asking them to walk naked down Main Street. But of course, I *am* asking them to do that. It's a requirement of any actor to walk naked down Main Street, and these guys will be no different. The scent of fear has crept into Room 15.

They don't know what I know. The safest place in the world is center stage. From the chilly wings, I waited for my cue, heard it, and ran into the hot light. The playwright gave me wit, the designer draped my body in silk, and a wig master had woven tresses to drip down my shoulders. I was more beautiful, classy, and smart than I could ever hope to be in real life. The audience, deep in blackness, stopped rustling, and waves of liquid love poured like a tsunami toward the stage in a wondrous bath.

For an actor, this is when the addiction begins.

But, these kids don't know this. Yet.

"Right now, we're deep breathing. Eyes closed, inhale—"

"But, but, but, Ms. Ryane . . ."

"Hold . . . hold . . . hold . . . and exhale." I stay the course and some—a couple, maybe one—follow along.

"Grace, would you like to demonstrate Child's Pose?" I ask.

Delighted to be picked, Grace drops to the floor, throws her arms forward, and touches her forehead in front of her knees. Perfect. Stella, Azra, Carla, and Jennifer join in. Marin slides off her chair and kneels, but she won't participate.

"The Shakespeare Club has rules," I say as I pace behind them and in front of them. Up one side and down the other. As long as I keep moving, they have to twist and turn to follow me.

"Rule one: do not even bother asking me to go to the bathroom or get water. There will be one five-minute break every meeting to do that."

I hold up a small wooden rattle and shake it. "This sound means get the hell back here fast."

"Whoa, Ms. Ryane, whoa, whoa, you can't cuss. You can't use bad words in front of us—we're kids." Candace's face is a mask of dismay.

"Right, okay, sorry about that." I wrack my brain. What did I say? Is *hell* a bad word? I guess it is. I forget because it's been misplaced in my vast lexicon of profanity.

"So, the break is five—"

"But you really *can't* say that!" Jordan, Candace's sister, cuts me off.

"Got it. I believe you. Relax." They're ready to fingerprint me and take my mug shot. "Rule two: I'm the only one who writes on the board. You can stop fighting over the markers because you will not be writing on the board."

The whiteboard markers are gold booty in a classroom. Grabbing one and scribbling with it is tantamount to winning an Olympic medal. Maybe it makes a kid feel like an adult.

"Rule three: do not talk when someone else is talking or reading aloud. I need to see some serious focus in this room, and it's rude to speak over other people."

Beats me if they hear this, as their eyes are on the jar of markers. They're calculating how to score the damn things. *Damn*, bad word, right?

"Rehearsing a play requires discipline and the ability to take direction. You'll have to prove you can do that."

"How do we prove that, Ms. Ryane?" Anna twirls her ever-present pink boa.

Thank the Lord, someone hears me.

"You can prove it by listening and doing as you're asked."

Anna, her brow furrowed, considers this. She casts a look over the group.

"I think we can do this," she announces.

"I'm thrilled to hear your confidence, Anna, and I agree with you."

Miles sucks on the end of his sleeve, staring at the colored markers on the whiteboard ledge.

"Miles, do you think we can do this?"

He blinks as if waking from a nap. He shrugs.

"We have one more meeting before winter break"—*can't say Christmas, don't say Christmas*—"and at that meeting, you will get three things."

Now I have their attention. Even Miles rocks forward in his chair. Getting stuff is big with kids. It doesn't matter *what* stuff, just stuff.

"One: you will each receive your very own script of the play, *A Midsummer Night's Dream*."

The kids snicker and roll their eyes. When did they become cynical?

"Two: you will each get a gift."

"What?"

"What!"

They pop up and down like exploding kernels.

"It's a surprise, and I'm not telling. And three: we'll have a party."

Their whoops and cheers fill the room, and I write the three things on the board:

1. SCRIPT
2. GIFT
3. PARTY

"Here's the thing, my kiddiewinks: if any *one* of you breaks a rule, I'll cross something off this list and *everyone* loses that thing. You'll have to earn it back."

They're quiet and still. Bribery. So far, so good. We can begin.

I've made laminated placards with the names of various characters in Shakespeare's life. Each card has a piece of green wool for hanging over a tiny neck. Someone will be WILLIAM; another, his wife, ANNE HATHAWAY; others, his parents, his three children, and— the most coveted role— QUEEN ELIZABETH.

We're about to read aloud the story of Shakespeare's life from *A Child's Portrait of Shakespeare*, a book by Lois Burdett, a Canadian teacher who had great success teaching the Bard to second graders. Suffice it to say, I'm aquiver in jealousy at her ability, but I manage to push the green-eyed monster aside for the moment.

"Shakespeare's father was a glover. Does anyone have an idea what that job might be?"

"He made gloves?"

"Exactly, Anna. And what do you think William, his parents, and the towns-people did for fun in those days?"

I get shrugs.

"Remember we talked about this a couple of weeks ago?"

"Played soccer?" Miles asks.

"Yes, they did kick a ball, and they played card games, but the big event was always when the players came to town."

"The soccer players?" Miles again.

"No, the actors." I hold up a picture of Elizabethan actors in a horse-drawn cart with citizens chasing after them. "Actors came to town to perform plays. But remember, no girls. Girls weren't allowed to act or even to go to school."

"What did they do?" Candace asks.

"They had to stay home sewing and cooking. In those days, it was thought that all women could do was cook and sew and have babies. It wasn't like today."

"Boys rule!" Daniel shouts.

"It was no picnic for the boys either. Until they turned seven, boys had to wear dresses."

The girls roar with laughter. Daniel and Miles look humiliated, as if they themselves were wearing dresses.

"It's true. When a boy turned seven, his family had a big party for him, and he got his first pair of pants, or breeches. The event was called a "breeching party.""

Daniel and Miles look as if they've been asked to eat mud.

"School was very difficult for Elizabethan boys, with long days starting at six in the morning. If a boy did anything wrong, he was beaten with a stick by the headmaster. Boys had to study Latin and astronomy and—get this—dancing."

"Dancing!" Daniel screams. "Are you for real?"

"I am for very real."

On the board: irony.

"Here's a new word for you. When we work on A Midsummer Night's Dream, you girls will be playing some of the male characters."

A collective "whaaaaat?"

"Look around you. We only have two boys, and most of the parts Shakespeare wrote were for boys." I point to the new word. "So, this is what I mean by *irony*. Girls, this is your time in the sun."

The girls groan. My news does not have the desired effect.

"No, pleeease, nooooo," Stella moans. "Do you mean we won't even wear dresses? We have to look like boys?"

They don't see this as a glorious time. They want to wear makeup and dresses and sparkles.

"When William Shakespeare was a teenager, he had a girlfriend, and for dates he had to walk over a mile to her farm, which was called Shottery. The girl's name was Anne Hathaway. Here's a picture of her house. It's still there . . . cute, right?"

"Anne Hathaway?" Candace calls out.

"Yes."

"She was in *Princess Diaries*," Stella whoops.

"She's so pretty," Jennifer adds.

"That's William Shakespeare's girlfriend?" Regina asks.

"No, different Anne Hathaway. Remember this was a long, long time ago?"

"Oh, yeah," Stella says, disappointed. "She's cool, though."

"Daniel, why don't you read the part of William Shakespeare? Stella, you read the part of Anne Hathaway. Carla, would you please read Queen Elizabeth?"

No way. Carla cowers in her chair, wildly shaking her head side to side and holding onto the edges of her seat as if a tornado might pull her away.

"That's okay, Carla. Maybe next time."

Dana waves her arm madly. She stands and dwarfs the kids around her.

"Please, please, Ms. Ryane. Can I, please?"

"Okay, Dana, go for it."

"Ms. Ryane?"

"Yes, Dana?"

"Can my mom make us a party after we do the play? Like at the end of it?"

"Gosh, that would be lovely. But for one thing, we haven't even *read* the play yet, let alone rehearsed the play, and *if* we do it, the performance wouldn't be until next May and we're only in early December. Do you see where I'm going with this? Planning a party seems slightly ahead of ourselves, but we can certainly keep it in mind."

Daniel flips the pages of his book. Then he holds it up over his face and creates a private office where he can chat with Miles.

"Daniel?"

He lowers the book so I can only see his eyes.

"Are you with us?"

He throws himself to the floor and rolls around on the carpet.

I don't know why he does this. It's weird, as if a lunatic madness has instantly possessed him. I can't figure it out. Moments like this catch me off-guard. I don't understand the physical compulsion of a fourth-grade boy to fly through the air, land with a crash, and laugh maniacally.

"Daniel, can you please begin reading? You need to sit up."

He kneels and straightens up, opens his mouth, gets two words out, and falls again to the floor, screaming.

"Is there a problem?"

He gathers himself, starts to speak, and collapses, giggling like a drunk. Then he doesn't say anything at all. In the silence, I stare at him, unsure of what to say. What's wrong?

"This is too much!" he cries.

"What do you mean? Should someone else read the part?"

"No, no . . . I'll do it," he answers loudly, as if doing me a great favor.

"Then let's hear it, and I suggest you sit in your chair."

In my periphery, I spy Miles. He's crawled to the whiteboard, lifted the marker jar off the ledge, and is about to extricate the blue one.

"Are you sure you want to do that, Miles?"

He shrugs, replaces the marker in the jar with a clink, and snakes his way back to us on his stomach. He weaves across the floor, using his elbows to propel him forward. He covers the whole carpet map, edging along the U.S.-Canada border, and arrives at his chair with a proud flourish. Stunned, I rub my eyes.

"Daniel, please read."

Instead, Daniel screeches and points at me.

"What now?"

"Ahhh . . . Ms. Ryane, check it out." Daniel gestures to his own eyes and back to me, and I remember the mascara I'd applied . . . what . . . minutes, hours, days ago?

"Eeew!" he adds.

"Fine, got it, thank you very much." I grab my purse for a fingerful of cream to clean my face. "Funny, funny, I know. Let's start."

Daniel launches, "A boy . . . was born . . . in . . . England. . . ." And he's off again, guffawing, burying his face in his hands and rolling on the floor.

"Okay, Daniel." I go to the board and swipe number two off the prize list. "You just lost that gift. For the whole group."

"What?" He stares with his mouth open.

"Rules, remember?" I give him a long look. "We can't even dream of doing a play if this is how you behave, Daniel. Everyone here is waiting for you to read and you want to act crazy."

"Awww . . ." The group turns on Daniel like a pack of coyotes.

"Daniel, you wrecked it," Marin states with arms crossed.

"You lost the gift, *Daniel*," Stella spits.

"But—but—Ms. Ryane," he protests, "you could keep *my* gift but don't make *everyone* lose it!"

"Nope. Everyone, Daniel." I shake my head. "You lost the gift for the group, and you have the rest of today and the beginning of the next meeting to earn it back. Good luck with that."

Daniel yanks a handful of dollar bills from his pants pocket and thrusts it at me.

"Here. You can have this."

Bribery. From a nine-year-old. He's put us on a two-way street.

"Keep your money. Next week you'll have a chance to redeem yourself."

Daniel puts the hush money away.

"Journals. Sit where they're placed and write about Shakespeare's girlfriend, or the queen, or the players that came to town."

Daniel's forehead is in his hand as he doodles in his notebook. Seated next to him, Marin gives him a sharp elbow to the ribs. I squeeze between them and sit.

"Daniel, you're a bright fellow. What would you like to write about?"

"I don't know," he mumbles.

"Here's a thought. Why don't you write as if you were a boy a long time ago. And you had to go to school so early it was still dark out. You had to study Latin, and dancing, and all about the stars. Write about what that feels like."

"Yeah. How much longer, Ms. Ryane?"

It's been a rough day.

"Just a few more minutes." I pat him on the shoulder.

As I move away, I'm tackled in an embrace from Carla. Her head comes to my waist, and her arms are tight around my legs.

"Well heck, Carla. What's this for?"

"You didn't make me read," she beams.

"I'll never make you do that, Carla." I brush the bangs from her eyes. She moves away, leaving Cheeto fingerprints on my cords. An affectionate tattoo.

At four o'clock, the kids run off, fighting over Cheeto remains. They slam out the door, and I pick up chairs and poke through a few journals. Daniel's journal is close to empty, with only blue and black circles filling two pages.

"Ms. Ryane, can I help you clean up?"

"That would be great, Azra." And we pack away pencils and books.

"I am going on a trip, but first I will be here for the celebration." Azra's eyes shine through her glasses. She calls our party a "celebration" and hops from one foot to the other, excited to share this news with me.

"Where are you going, Azra?"

"I am going to Florida and Antarctica," she sings.

"Wow, that's some trip. You're going to be both very hot and very cold."

"I know, and I'm getting a new dress because we're going to a wedding!"

Azra's mom pops her head in the door.

"Azra was just telling me about the big trip."

"Oh, yes," she grins. "My brother-in-law is getting married. It's very exciting, and the wedding festivities will take all week."

"Will that be in Florida or Antarctica?"

"Florida," she says with a puzzled look.

Azra beams at me with those big blues.

"Of course, Florida. Silly me." I touch Azra on the back as if to signal, *Your secret is safe with me.* "See you next week, Azra."

She waves and runs off.

I'm not sure why Azra wants me to think she's going to Antarctica. Maybe she wants to impress me. Maybe she has a fantasy of going to Antarctica. Maybe her class is studying Antarctica. Whatever the case, I love hearing her say it with such wholehearted belief. Let's all go to Antarctica.

As I cross the school grounds, someone shouts, "Bye, Mel!"

Marin, all alone in the courtyard, has her arm raised in a farewell salute.

I smile and wave. This girl marches to her own drummer, and I have to learn her beat.

"See ya, Marin," I call back. Maybe I can slip her a buck to call me "Ms. Ryane."

CHILDREN'S WRITES

Dear journal,
*   My dad cut my mom's head off. I am so mad about that. I am so*
angry. They say I have to get married but I am never going to marry
anyone because a man could do that to you.
Queen Elizabeth

LESSON PLAN

Say what you mean and mean what you say. Always. Most of the time. As much as possible. Try your best.

I find Marin's fourth-grade teacher. "Can you tell me a little something about Marin?" I ask.

"Sure, is there a problem?"

"Well, I'm not sure . . . she's disruptive. She particularly likes to provoke the boys in the group, and I was just wondering how she is in your class."

"She's been fine with me, but if she's causing trouble, kick her out."

The idea of kicking someone out of the club spells failure to me. It's draconian. The teacher continues, "If you like, I can talk to her grandmother about it. She's very supportive of the school."

"Who's her grandmother?"

"Helen."

"Helen, Grace's mother?"

"That's the one. Helen is Grace's mom and Marin's grandmother. Marin has three sisters and a single mother. There are four fathers for those four girls."

My head spins, trying to keep the facts straight. Small wonder Marin is acting out.

"Thanks so much."

I stumble to my car. I feel blind and more than a little naive, and I don't know what to do.

A few days later, I run into Helen. She's sweet and amazingly calm, considering she runs quite a houseful.

"I talked with Marin," she says.

"Oh, okay." I have a twinge of guilt for the chat I had with Marin's teacher.

"I told her it is an honor to be in the Shakespeare Club, and she must have more respect."

"Wow, that's great. Any chance you could talk to all of them?"

Helen smiles. She's warm. I want to go home with her. I wish she were my mom or grandma or aunt or my somebody.

"Helen, do you think Marin is a bit angry?"

"Yes." Helen nods. "I think she is."

"We'll work it out, don't worry. And thanks again."

I'm not sure how I'm going to make it happen, but I want to make it work for Marin and me.

Back home, I try to figure out the relationship between Grace and Marin. I draw a chart, putting in stick figures of Helen, her daughter, her daughter's child, Marin, and Helen's child, Grace.

Grace is eight and Marin is nine. Grace is Marin's aunt.

CHAPTER IV

PARTY TO THE PARTY

> Whiles you are willing it shall come to note,
> What time we will our celebration keep...
>
> *Twelfth Night* Act IV, Scene III

I catch up with Marin on the quad, and we make our way toward Room 15. She struggles with what appears to be a sixty-pound backpack.

"Need help?" I ask.

"Nope," she answers, curt.

I put my arm around her shoulders.

"Well, I could use your help." I give her a squeeze.

"With what?" She stops and pulls away from me.

"Marin, I think you have leadership qualities. I need someone who can set the pace for the others, and I think you might be that kind of person."

She doesn't answer; she takes off, dragging the heavy backpack in the dirt. I tag along, trying to figure her out. I'd worked on that little speech, and it meant nothing to her.

Don't kid a kidder. She obviously knows I've spoken with both her teacher and her grandmother. Is she pissed off at me? Does she feel betrayed?

Later, inside Room 15, another voice pipes up. "Ms. Ryane?"

"Yes, Regina?"

"Daniel is sick."

"Okay, thanks." I put an *X* next to his name. Very convenient, Daniel. Couldn't buy your way out of earning back the gift, so you got sick.

I address the kids. "William Shakespeare married Anne Hathaway, and they had three children: Susanna and the twins, Hamnet and Judith."

I imagine it was Shakespeare's burning ambition that sent him to London in pursuit of a theatrical career. Or did he marry too young? Was he bored with small-town life and a wife and three kids? History is hazy on these points. In any case, he split. "He made the long journey from Stratford to the polluted and overcrowded city of London."

"Like, you mean, smog?" Candace asks.

"So much smog," I confirm.

"Like Los Angeles."

I address Candace's lookalike. "Jordan, do you think Shakespeare knew he was talented and went to the big city to become a star?"

"I don't know," Jordan shrugs.

"Anyone have thoughts about this?" Eleven faces stare at me.

"Was he having an affair?" Dana asks.

An affair? Where did that come from?

"I don't think so, Dana. Why do you ask?"

She doesn't answer.

"He did have three children with Anne. I think he loved her," I say.

Actually, some scholars believe Shakespeare wasn't so enamored of his wife. He died a wealthy man, but in his will, all William left to Anne was their marriage bed. That's quite a statement from a man who was never at a loss for words. A piece of furniture, a bed in which he spent very little time, from the genius who wrote great romances. Pretty damn cold.

Three children, huddled together on a linoleum kitchen floor, watched their mother, wild and crazed, swing a broom at their father's head.

She railed at him, "Bastard!"

He ducked, flew at her, grabbed her by the hair, and dragged her outside into the icy night. She screamed, flailed, and kicked, and he slammed the door. From outside, she banged and banged and banged.

"Please don't, Daddy—please stop!" the little boys cried.

Daddy, fed up and exhausted, fell into a chair. Mommy burst back through the door, sobbing, and grappled at her husband. She scratched and assailed. She kicked the broom and sent it across the room.

"Please . . . please, Mommy, don't . . ." The small voices, ignored, faded away.

I held those little boys close and led them to another room, away from the desperate display of a worn-out marriage. We were a tightly gathered three-some on a weathered couch. I wiped tear-stained cheeks and runny noses with the sleeve of my flannel pajamas. I was nine.

"Does that mean he had to do his business three times?" Marin asks.

"What business?" I have no idea what she's talking about.

"His business." She looks around the room, and the giggles start.

"What do you mean, Marin?"

"His *business* . . . to get those kids?" she answers, a little too loud.

"Yes, I suppose he did. At least twice, anyway."

Jordan and Candace slouch in their seats. This discussion of Shakespeare disappearing on his family seems not to hold their interest. I learned from their teacher that their mother had recently left the family. She abandoned them and two older sisters to be taken care of by their father. Perhaps too much interest is at stake for these twins.

"My dad is sad," Candace tells me. "He got hurt at work and has to have a cane."

"Gosh, that must be rough on all of you."

I imagine the poor fellow limping around a house with no partner and four daughters to care for. Perhaps this was how Anne Hathaway felt when her young husband took off for worlds unknown. Who did she talk to? Her in-laws, with whom she shared a crowded cottage? Her desolation would have plunged to new lows when her eleven-year-old son, Hamnet, died, perhaps of the Black Death or possibly by drowning in the Avon River—no one is certain. 'Tis another point historians cannot verify.

Candace wears her blue and white BABY GIRL satin jacket. She'll wear this piece of clothing for the entire school year. Two seats away, her twin, Jordan, hugs her chest with arms crossed tight. She's in a black hoodie, a jacket she'll wear for the rest of the school year. Their teacher believes Jordan is in mourning.

"Big day today," I announce. "Our party and our gifts."

Room 15 is abuzz.

"And," I attempt to top the commotion, "another new rule. What do you suppose this means?" I raise my arm.

"Be quiet?" Stella shouts.

"Exactly, Stella. Be quiet. Not a word when my arm goes up. I'll wait however long it takes for silence to reign."

"Until it rains?" Carla screams.

"Just think of me as the Queen, Carla. I'm reigning over you and waiting for the silence of my court."

"It's not me that talks," Stella cries.

"It is too," Jennifer yells.

"You never stop!" Regina adds.

"No, no, not always me! No, Ms. Ryane!" Stella protests.

My arm is raised. They don't notice. Utterly useless. In fact, it's up so long that it starts to ache. I have to support it with my other arm as the noise escalates.

I drop my head back, letting it hang as I stare at the ceiling. This can't possibly be happening in every classroom. *What do I not know?* I look back at them, and they're on their feet, pushing each other and screeching.

All but one.

Marin studies me and my upraised arm. She has the quiet demeanor of a diplomat. She squints at me. She's composed, as if figuring something out.

"You guys!" she bursts out. "Hey, you guys! We're not going to have our party if you don't listen!"

Anna quits fighting for her stolen chair and joins Marin's argument. "Hey, yeah, stop—stop, everyone—quiet! Quiet! We won't get our party, you guys!"

The shuffling ends, and everyone takes a seat. Silence.

"Good. Thank you, Marin and Anna, for modeling leadership under duress." I massage my sore arm.

Strolling behind them, I whisper, "Deep breaths, eyes closed." Marin's eyes are wide open; I give her a nod, and she lets her eyes droop closed for the first time.

"That's it, big breath in . . . hold it . . . hold it . . . and exhale—"

"Are we having a celebration today?" Azra asks, breaking the peace.

"Yes, but first, we're going to learn an actor's preparation with a vocal warm-up. Real actors exercise their voices to act onstage, and that's what we're going to do."

Without warning, Carla screams at the top of her lungs. She shrieks, stunning me and everyone else. Good God, where did that come from? Her chubby arms are stretched to the ceiling. Just as abruptly, she freezes, drops her arms, and blinks at us as if woken from a dream.

"Carla?"

She busts out chortling, as does everyone else.

I'm stupefied, as Room 15 becomes Havana, Cuba, circa New Year's Eve in 1948. It's a party. It's ridiculous, and I hold my sides laughing. The kids leap out of their chairs and join me in convulsing with giddy mayhem. My tears of laughter create a blurry picture of twelve children howling and bobbing up and down in their seats.

Ah, let the merrymaking begin: it's been a long time coming to Shakespeare Club. Rules be damned. The absurdity of Carla's reaction to the idea of a vocal warm-up is the kind of nuttiness we need to share.

"That's good, Carla," I squeak. "Does this mean you might read aloud in the near future?"

She adamantly shakes her head. No way.

"Okay, no pressure." I take her face in my hands and give her a big hug. "Carla, I'm plain crazy about you."

I gesture for the kids to stand and they do. "Squeeze your shoulders up high to your ears and let them drop like weights. Good . . . up . . . up again . . . and let them drop. Now pretend your tongue is a bumblebee in your mouth, flying in and out of every nook and cranny, hiding behind your teeth and in your cheeks and under your tongue while you hum."

Like a beehive, we buzz together. Even Miles joins in. It's the first time we have cohesion. For one silly, sparkling moment, we're one, and I see that we're capable of accomplishing something. All because of the zany outburst of a funny little girl.

"We're going to play a game." This causes smiles throughout the room. I pull out a paper lunch bag.

"Who wants to go first?"

Hands fly up. They have no idea what this game is, but being first is important.

"Okay, Grace, pick someone you'd like to insult." Grace scans the group and looks at Carla.

"Take a card." Grace reaches into the bag and pulls out a note card. She runs to Carla and peers at the card. Bewildered, she looks back at me.

"Come here, I'll help you."

Inside the bag are note cards with Shakespearean curses taken from his plays. I whisper in Grace's ear and send her back to Carla, where she shifts her weight from one foot to the other. She checks with me.

"You can do it. It'll be fun. Use your big voice."

Out comes a tiny peep. "You . . . you . . . " She glances back at me and shakes her head.

"Try again, bigger voice. This is your chance to really give Carla an insult."

"You . . . you stale old mouse-eaten cheese!"

A pause, then Carla bursts out laughing. Grace, realizing she's hilarious, joins in and soon, other hands are in the air begging to be picked. They want to shout these saucy abuses at each other.

"Thou crusty botch of nature."

"You viperous worm that gnaws at the bowels."

"Thou liest, thou shag-eared villain."

"You peddler's excrement."

"Thou drone, thou snail, thou slug, thou sot."

"King urinal—King mockwater."

"What is that? What does that mean?" Miles asks.

"A urinal is where men pee."

Shrieks of "men pee!" fill Room 15.

One after another, the kids step up to use words they'd never heard, much less spoken. One after another, they struggle to use their big voices.

Carla and Azra are the last two up. Azra reaches into the bag with caution, as if a live animal might be inside. She struggles to make sense of what she reads. I whisper the insult into her ear and give her a tiny push toward Miles. She can't look right at Miles's face, but she manages to squeak out, "You poisonous bunch-back'd toad."

Carla cannot bring herself to do it. She holds on tight to her chair.

"That's okay, Carla, maybe someday. You did show us your big voice once today, and that was pretty impressive."

"Make her, make her!" they cry.

"We don't *make* people stand up in front of others in Shakespeare Club."

"Ms. Ryane?" Anna's hand is up. "When's our party?"

"Soon, our party is soon, but first our journals."

They run to their journals laid out on the tables and start switching places.

"No, no, no, stay where your journals are!"

Too late. I can't keep up with them, they scatter so fast. I can't even remember where I originally put them. Right on the heels of bonding, they separate into the dreaded cliques. Miles is under a table. I crawl under there with him.

"You need to do your journal work, Miles. You need to begin doing as you're told."

He shrugs.

"Miles, seriously . . . the gifts and party are in your hands." He doesn't move.

"You have to ask yourself, Miles, if you can live with losing everything for the group, because you're very close to accomplishing that."

Miles gives my threat some thought and crawls out. He draws an action figure in his journal. It's a pretty good action figure. It has nothing to do with anything in the Shakespeare Club and everything to do with being a boy.

"Girls, you might want to write about not being allowed to go to school. What it would be like to have to stay home and learn sewing and cooking."

They draw Elizabeth I. She's always in pink and purple. She's always smiling and dripping with jewelry. She'd fit right in on Rodeo Drive.

I hand each child a new pen wrapped in a glittering gold ribbon and a candy cane. This is the promised gift. Now they'll each have a special pen for journal writing.

"Party time!" I pile a mountain of cookies on a big red paper plate beside a tub of red and green jelly candies. I hand out juice boxes.

I also distribute the third part of my bribe, but the children flip through binders of my adapted *A Midsummer Night's Dream* and toss them aside.

"After the winter break, please, *please* remember to bring these scripts with you. We'll start reading the play in January."

They bob their heads, but they can't speak with cheeks puffed full of cookies and candy. Within four minutes, the food has been grabbed, stuffed in pockets, and crammed into mouths. Gone. The fastest party on record.

"Thank you, Ms. Ryane."

"Thank you, Ms. Ryane."

"Thank you, Ms. Ryane. . . ." Their voices echo out the door and into the schoolyard. Gone, all gone, with a mess of crumbs, crayons, and journals as the only evidence of their presence. Chairs lie tipped over.

I could write a book on the art of throwing a ten-minute party.

Carla, almost out the door, returns. She saunters over and tilts her head up. I fasten onto her brown eyes and wonder what's on her mind.

"Ms. Ryane?"

"Yup, Carla?"

She screws up her face. "Ms. Ryane, why did you say that thing . . . that thing that you were crazy about me?"

"Well, Carla, because I *am* crazy about you. I think you're terrific."

"Okay." And she wanders toward the exit.

As she gets to the door, she looks back. "Have a nice Christmas, Ms. Ryane."

"You too, Carla. See you next year."

I'm cleaning up the party mess when I notice Azra standing alone. She's clutching her script and the golden bow with her pen and candy cane.

"Are you going to help me, Azra?"

"Yes," she chirps.

We pick up chairs and fill the trash.

"Ms. Ryane?"

"Yes?"

"I like Shakespeare Club." She fills a Ziploc bag with colored pens.

"What do you like about it?"

"I like Queen Elizabeth!"

"Yes, you really do. I've noticed your journal is filled with drawings of her. Azra, look, it's your mom."

Azra grabs her pink backpack.

"Have a wonderful trip," I say as they leave.

Azra runs back and throws her arms around my legs. I take her face in my hands. "Really, have a good time, my sweet. I'll be here when you get back."

I would never see Azra again.

CHILDREN'S WRITES

Dear jirnal,

Queen Elizabeth was a good queen. She was so nice people love her. William Shakespeare went to London because I like his plays. William Shakespeares son died when he was 11 year old. But William was in London his wife write a litter to him was that his son died.

LESSON PLAN

Ask, ask, ask. Three years later, during a casual conversation with another teacher, I learned that Daniel could barely read and had been failed upward. He hadn't been rolling around, laughing in joy. The boy had been in a state of terror.

I drive away from the school, delighted to start a three-week break. At home, curled in an armchair, I stare into space with the cat purring in my lap. When William walks in, I fill him in.

"As parties go, you would have liked it. Very quick, with excellent food, excellent drink, and not a lot of chitchat."

William smiles.

"I guess I'll go back. I mean, I think they like it. It might work out—we'll see."

"You sound very committed."

"You know, the Elizabethans didn't have very clean drinking water and depended on ale to satisfy their thirst."

"I think we should start the winter break as Elizabethans."

I drop into Arden Street before classes end for winter break. I want to leave Daniel's unclaimed gifts in his teacher's mailbox. Instead, I discover him on a cot in the school office.

"Daniel, what's going on?" I sit beside him. He looks droopy and weak.

"I got really tired and kinda felt sick."

"Hmmm, that's too bad. Well, I'm glad I ran into you because you were away for the last Shakespeare Club meeting, and I wanted you to have your gifts."

I hand him the book, pen, and candy cane. He takes them and lays his head down again.

"Daniel, I want you to think about something over the break, okay?"

He nods.

"Shakespeare Club isn't like a class. You don't get grades, you don't pass or fail, and it's not something you have to do. Do you know what I mean?"

He rests his head on his hands, looks at me, and nods. I touch his shoulder.

"Daniel, I'm not sure this is a program that really interests you. You have a lot of physical energy, and I'm thinking you might be happier playing soccer or just running around after school and not learning about Shakespeare because, like I said, you don't really have to do this."

He pops up. "No, no, I want to do Shakespeare Club. I do—really."

"Well, okay then, but you have to change. I'm being straight up about this. You have to figure out how to focus and not act crazy."

He lays his head back down.

"I'll see you in the New Year. Give it some thought."

"Bye, Ms. Ryane."

"See ya, Daniel, feel better. The candy cane might help."

Chapter V

WINTER BREAKDOWN

The wall is high, and yet will I leap down.
Good ground, be pitiful and hurt me not!
King John Act IV, Scene III

"We went to Mexico!"

"I got fifty dollars!"

"My sister got pneumonia!"

"Nothing fun. Christmas was a dud," Jordan says.

"We went to my grandma's in Oxnard. It was okay. My dad is still sad," Candace adds.

"So. William Shakespeare began his career in London as a water boy. He was a gofer to the actors and directors. Does anybody know what that means, to be a gofer?"

"Like a squirrel?" Carla asks.

"A little bit. William Shakespeare's career started at the very bottom. He had to run around getting stuff for the stars. If an actor wanted a sandwich, Shakespeare got it. If a director wanted a drink, Shakespeare got it. And all the time, he watched and listened and learned about the theatre."

In the palm of my eight-year-old hand was a silver cylinder. The top was a perfect replica of a nickel. Black lines painted on its sides made the cylinder appear to be a stack of nickels. A crowd of kids gathered around me on the gravel schoolyard. Rain poured down on us, and my glasses were foggy, but who cared: today I was a star with my magic disappearing nickel trick. The kids elbowed each other to get in close and watch as, over and over, I made a nickel disappear.

"How'd she do that?"

"Let me see!"

"Hey, kid, give that to me!"

I snapped my hand closed, and a big boy shoved his face into mine.

"I said hand it over!" he shouted.

I shook my head and swiped rain from my glasses. He tried to get my arm from behind my back, but I pulled away hard. No one was taking my trick. No one was yanking my act.

"Leave her alone! C'mon, let's see it again!"

Other kids pushed in front of the bully and clamored for another look-see at the magic. It was a cheap little magic trick my dad had brought home for me. I loved my dad for that. I was an outsider in misty glasses, and suddenly, I was inside. I was cool, fast, and interesting.

Rain soaked my shoes and hair and wool sweater, but I smelled fame.

"After his fantastic career as an actor and success as a playwright, Shakespeare came home to Stratford-upon-Avon to retire and to see his daughters marry. He died on April 23," I tell the kids, "and here's what's strange: April 23 was also his . . . what?"

"His birthday?" Anna calls out, flipping her pink boa.

"Excellent, Anna, for remembering that." I give her a wink. "And I want you all to know that when we get to April 23, we'll be celebrating Shakespeare's birthday."

This has become my habit. Whenever frenzy or boredom overtakes Room 15, I promise a party. Don't all teachers do this?

"Pizza!" Marin yells.

"Yeah, pizza!" Miles agrees.

"Ms. Ryane! Let's have pizza!" Stella cries, as if this were an original thought.

Daniel doesn't say anything because he hasn't returned to us after winter break.

"Pizza is under consideration; however, I would like to point out that April 23 is a far cry from January, where we are today, and we have much to do before then."

On the board: READ-THROUGH.

"Let's begin reading the play."

"I wanna be a faaaiiirrry!" Stella cries.

"I wanna be a girl!" Dana shouts.

"Me too!" Jordan chants. "Girl, girl, girl!"

"I don't want to be nothin'," Carla declares.

"You don't even know these characters or the story!" I say way too loud. I swallow and try again softly. "We can't fight about casting until we've read the play. So let's do that."

"But, I'm booorrred, and I want to play a giiirrrlll," Stella whines. I answer her with a grimace and a shake of my head.

"Look, if you guys don't give a damn about doing this, then I won't either."

"Awww, Ms. Ryane—whoa, whoa, you can't say that—you can't cuss—you can't talk like that." Candace is all over me.

"Right, right. Forget it, let's start."

"But seriously, Ms. Ryane, you can't use bad words with us." Her look is scathing. Ready to shatter glass.

"Candace, I got it. We're moving on." My shoulders feel slumped to my knee-caps. "So, Hermia's dad wants her to marry Demetrius, but she wants to marry Lysander. Her father gives her three options: marry the boy he's chosen, go live in a convent, or die."

"*Die?*" Marin asks.

"Yup, he'll have her killed."

"Cool," Marin says.

"What's a . . . con . . . con . . . ?" Grace searches her script.

"Convent?" I ask, and she nods. "A convent is where nuns live."

Their looks are vacant.

"Do you guys know what a nun is?"

"Nope," Carla answers.

"A nun is a woman who decides to give up regular life and dedicate herself to prayer and doing good things for people."

"Are you a nun, Ms. Ryane?" Regina asks.

Yes, I am.

"No, I am not. I'm not a nun. I'm married. Nuns don't have boyfriends or get married."

"How many kids do you have?" Marin demands.

"I don't have kids."

"Then why are you married?"

At nine, Marin may well be the youngest agent in the FBI.

"You don't have to have kids to be married," I say, a little defensively. "Frankly, you guys should be happy that I don't have kids. If I did, I wouldn't have time to have all this fun with you."

What they don't know is I've actually considered a life in Nunville. In search of a future after the end of my acting career, I entertained a number of ideas. Perhaps dressing in a uniform, eating three square meals a day, and sleeping in a castle-type joint was just what I was looking for. At Mass in just such a place, I prayed in a chapel filled with nuns. I was on a retreat to explore the monastic life.

As I knelt, a horrible ringing annulled the holy silence. I gritted my teeth and willed the cell phone in my purse to shut up. It didn't. I pounced on the bag to suffocate the damn thing. I dug for the phone, inadvertently dumping the contents of my purse onto the marble floor. Keys clanged, and a small pot of lip-gloss rolled under a pew, skimming along the shiny surface. I reached to grab it, but it was beyond me. The round plastic vessel halted at the black rubber heels of a nun.

I peeped over the top of the pew to see if she had noticed. Not a flinch. I slipped down and snaked my way under the pew to close my fingers over it. With stealthy care, like a Mata Hari, I tucked cosmetics, keys, and breath mints inside my bag and resumed the prayer position.

My heart thumped, and I wanted to weep. I couldn't even act like a nun.

At lunch, the nuns and I shared bologna sandwiches and sipped from small cartons of chocolate milk. I felt the need to explain my gauche behavior.

"I'm so sorry," I said as I tapped my mouth with a paper napkin. "I should have shut my phone off. That was awful." I wanted forgiveness, but they smiled and said nothing.

Later, I learned they were from the Philippines and didn't speak English.

The message on my phone turned out to offer another kind of life change. I'd been accepted into a prestigious directing program at the American Film Institute.

The nuns lined up to see me off, and I moved from one to another to say goodbye and thank them for my day. At the end of the row was an English-speaking nun. I was excited, bursting to tell someone about my phone call, so I spilled the news to her.

"I think this is what I'm supposed to do . . . film school," I gushed.

She gave me a hug and whispered in my ear, "You're going to be just fine. You're going to be a big success."

She was so confident. Maybe she was a psychic nun. She smiled and sent me on my way.

To this day, I keep the convent thing open. You never know.

I entered the AFI, brimming with joy and terror. I needed to raise money to make my film, and that frightened me. I would have to beg, which I found wholly distasteful. I was also nervous about heading up a crew and executing the project. But I was also imagining where this would take me. It simply had to mean I would find my future as a Hollywood director.

To date, that has not occurred. What did happen was a knock at my door and a meeting in my apartment kitchen with a man who wanted to edit my short film. I said okay.

As the project neared its completion, this same man told me he was going to kiss me. I said okay.

And on one hot summer night, he asked if I would marry him. I said okay.

Those were the three most important okays of my life. The nun was right. When William and I married, my life became a big success.

"In a convent, the nuns have to obey the Mother Superior and do everything they're told, whether they like it or not. Who here thinks they could live that life?"

"I could do it," Dana says with an air of peerless confidence, "but the little kids couldn't."

For Dana, all her classmates are "little kids." Dana's almost my height and surrounded by what she deems the favored and the cute, kids she thinks get away with murder.

Dana's thinking will be her undoing. Her ambition for popularity has set her on a rocky course. I keep my eye on her as she begins her mission of gossip mongering. She recruits other girls into a clique. This in-group bad-mouths others and plays games of deceit.

Dana and I will find ourselves engaged in an all-out war by May.

Two seats away from Dana, Anna munches on sunflower seeds. She bites, swallows, and spits shells into her hand. Like baby birds hungry for worms, the other kids stretch their palms toward Anna, begging for morsels. In a flash, Miles dives for the bag and rips it, scattering seeds all over the carpet, coast to coast.

"Okay, you have four minutes to gather up those seeds and shells and dump them in the garbage. All of you. Now. Go."

"But it was Miles who did it," Stella objects.

"Miles will help, but all of you will clean up. I'm counting, starting . . . NOW . . . GO!"

Sometimes I think if I say things loudly, action will follow.

They stare at me, unmoving.

"GO . . . GO . . . GO!"

Anna crouches and starts gathering errant shells. One after another, the girls follow her lead. Miles slinks off into a corner.

"Miles, you too. *Now*. Get to it."

Miles slouches, falls to the floor like a broken puppet, and picks up one seed, and one more, and . . . oh so slowly . . . one more. He's putting on a show, and I fume.

The noise in the room escalates. The kids run back and forth to the trash, deliberately crashing into each other. It's fun to mow someone down with your body. Screams of laughter top screams of pain, and I'm bewildered. I raise my arm for quiet. I wait. And wait. My arm trembles, and the chatter finally ends. They slither back into their chairs. Back to work.

"And what choice does Hermia make? She runs off into the forest with Lysander, her true love. Lysander is going to take her to his aunt's house, and they will secretly marry. But there's a problem: Lysander gets them lost."

"What a loser," Jordan says.

"Jordan, you have to imagine where they are when Lysander gets them lost. They've traveled in circles in a dark forest where, as it turns out, magical things happen. All they have to guide them is the light of the moon. It's an easy place to lose your way."

"What magical things?" Grace asks.

I snap my script closed and give them all a stern look.

"You tell me. Go home and read your scripts. Come back next week and tell me what happens next in the story."

"But, Ms. Ryane," Jennifer says, "it's not even four o'clock."

"Well, look at that, what do you know? You get out early. Swell . . . go on now . . . see ya next Thursday."

They're quiet. Dead still.

"Really, you can go now. That's all for today."

"Are you mad at us?" Marin asks.

"No, of course not," I say a tad too nicely.

Their penetrating looks tell me they aren't exactly buying this.

"Okay, here's the truth: I'm not very angry at you. A little bit, but not a lot. I just don't want to be a babysitter. That's not why I started Shakespeare Club, and today, that's what I feel like, so, you know, I hope next week'll be better."

Even Miles listens. His eyes are small slits. His look is unwavering. He makes me uncomfortable, and I fiddle with my fingers.

"I was an actor for a long time, and I got to do Shakespeare's plays. His plays are full of adventure, power, revenge, and love. Cool stuff like that. I want you to experience some of that."

Not a sound. Not a movement. Have I gone too far?

"Okay, look."

I yank a stack of 8" x 10" black-and-white photographs out of my binder. I spread them out on a table. The kids gather and study pictures of me as Olivia in *Twelfth Night*, Barbara in *Major Barbara*, Maggie in *Cat on a Hot Tin Roof*, and Mariana in *Measure for Measure*.

"You were in *Cat in the Hat*?" Carla asks.

"No, it's called *Cat on a Hot Tin Roof*."

"Was it like *Cat in the Hat*?"

"No, no hats at all. Look, here, I'm meeting the Queen of England after a command performance of a play called *You Never Can Tell*."

"You know Queen Elizabeth?" Stella asks.

"This is the second Queen Elizabeth. Shakespeare's queen was Elizabeth I. Different time. Do you get that? *Four hundred* years between them."

"How old are you, Ms. Ryane?" Carla asks.

"I'm a hundred."

"No, you're not! You're twenty-six or thirty-two," Jordan announces.

"Let's go with that."

"Ms. Ryane, you used to be so pretty," Regina says. *How darling.*

Marin nudges Regina hard. "What do you mean, *used to*? She's going to feel bad, like you think she looks ugly now."

Regina's jaw drops. "Oh, sorry, Ms. Ryane—I didn't—you know . . ."

"It's okay, Regina, I don't feel bad. Things change, people change, faces change. It's okay, really." I put my finger on her hand so she knows I mean it.

And I do. I don't want her to feel bad, but after they're gone, I pore over the photos and realize I *was* pretty, but I don't look like that anymore. The sad thing is, I didn't know it then. I never thought I was pretty, and I never thought I could be, and it's too bad because now it's too late to enjoy it.

"So, it's hard work," I say as I gather up the pictures, "and you have to decide if you're up for that. When we start rehearsing the play, you'll need to pay attention or else we'll never be able to do it."

"Are we going to have a real moon and a real forest?" Carla asks.

If only I could give them those.

"No, Carla, we won't have a real moon and a real forest. But we can be real people telling a fantastic story to an audience. People who don't know this story. And I promise you that'll be really fun."

A collective sigh. They're pretty much hoping for a real moon and a real forest. These kids have never seen a play, and I'm asking them to do Shakespeare. For them, a theater is a place that smells of stale popcorn.

"Alright, go on now. Give what I've said some thought and read your scripts. We'll try again next week."

"Thanks, Ms. Ryane, for doing this."

"You're welcome, Dana."

After they've left, I clean up alone. I'm on my hands and knees scrabbling for wayward sunflower seeds. I miss Azra. I wonder how her trip went and if she misses us. In the quiet, I sit back on my heels and dribble seeds from one hand to the other. I think about a nice vacation, lost in a forest, and what my life as a nun might have been like. I shake that nonsense out of my head. I'd make a lousy nun. I'd never be able to obey. Hell, I could never give up the damn swearing.

CHILDREN'S WRITES

Dear Diary,

If I were to be Hermia if they were to give me that same waring to be a nun—to die—or to marry Demetrius I would run away at night with my food and I would go away and never come back. I would find a place safe and quiet to live and one will find me because I will be in very far back into the woods safe.

LESSON PLAN

A smidgeon of fear can be a good and useful thing. Our principal taught me this when I worried, "I think they might be afraid to do the play, to be in front of people and to follow my lead."

"Fear is okay, Mel. Stick with it. Don't be afraid of their fear."

William and I spend Christmas in San Francisco. We check into a funky 1970s-style hotel overlooking the cliffs of the Sutro Baths. Our room is large and wood-paneled, with a brick wall housing a fireplace. Huge windows display a spectacular view of the coast. The ocean crashes against the rocky shore, and cypress trees shake in the wind. It is heaven. I love that we are in real weather. Mist and fog and rain spilling over a real city.

We stroll along the shore, balancing one foot after the other on rocky ledges while waves spray seawater at us. I think of poor King Lear screaming at the elements over which he's powerless.

Blow, winds, and crack your cheeks! rage, blow! . . .
Rumble thy bellyful! Spit, fire! Spout, rain! . . .
Then let fall
Your horrible pleasure. Here I stand your slave,
A poor, infirm, weak, and despis'd old man;
But yet I call you servile ministers . . .

It's clear to me what he's on about. I, too, am feeling poor, infirm, and weak. I can't get the gang of thirteen out of my head. Like the powerless King Lear, I feel at sea in a rickety boat attempting the impossible. Performing *A Midsummer Night's Dream*? I couldn't see how we'd get there.

Los Angeles is altogether too sunny and frustratingly unwalkable for my tastes. In San Francisco, William and I bundle up in coats and hats and head out for a romantic trek across the metropolis. We ride buses and cable cars to Fisherman's Wharf and hike back the entire length of the city to our hotel, a distance of over seven miles, window-shopping at mom-and-pop stores along the way. We peruse restaurant menus, ogle interesting architecture, and talk.

"I'm not sure I can finish it."

William puts his arm around my shoulders.

"I'm lousy at it, and they know it. They're on to me. Like I'm a fake teacher, and they can see right through me."

As darkness closes in, we stop at a cozy seafood restaurant. I sip crisp white wine and watch the other patrons engaged in chitchat.

"We should move here," I suggest.

"Here? Why?"

"Look at these people—they're content. I like this city. I bet I could accomplish things here. I could write a book, or a play, or make a movie . . . it just seems like that kind of place."

"Then that's what we'll do." William digs into his halibut.

"You're mocking me," I pout. "You're not being serious."

"*You're* not being serious." He points his knife at my salmon to get me eating.

"This is really good." I bite into the fish. "We could come here all the time if we lived here."

"So, how are you planning on starting the new year with the club?"

"We'll start rehearsals."

"Sounds good." He raises his wine glass. "Happy New Year!"

"Are you still making fun of me?"

"Never."

I ask Azra's third-grade teacher for information. Azra had gone to the wedding in Florida, but that trip was followed by another one. Azra and her family were on the *Hajj* pilgrimage to Mecca. Was Mecca Azra's Antarctica?

Tina, her teacher, looks worried. "I don't know if you've seen the news," she says.

All able-bodied Muslims are required to make one of these journeys during their lifetime. As the Muslim population grows, more and more people are making the trip, but the infrastructure has not been made safer for the participants. On the final day of the pilgrimage, after days of praying, a stoning ceremony takes place. Rocks are thrown at three stone pillars that represent the site where the devil is thought to have appeared to Abraham. The location of this ritual is across a narrow bridge. Over two million worshippers carrying rocks crowd onto the overpass, attempting to reach the other side.

In 1990, 1,426 pilgrims were crushed to death in a stampede. In 2004, over two hundred were trampled.

The year of Azra's journey, 345 would meet their demise on the overstuffed causeway, with almost three hundred injured. Where was little Azra in all this? Was she still dreaming of being Queen Elizabeth?

After a few more weeks of missing Azra, I return to Tina and learn that Azra and her family have arrived safely back in the U.S.

"Her parents came by and picked up Azra's belongings. They've moved away, I think, to the Valley."

She dreamed of Antarctica, but the hot, dry San Fernando Valley had taken Azra. If I didn't hate the desert before, I did now.

CHAPTER VI

WITS' WITLESS END

What? were you snarling all before I came,
Ready to catch each other by the throat,
And turn you all your hatred now on me?

Richard III Act I, Scene III

I run around the schoolyard, tying bits of green yarn around each club member's wrist. This is a reminder to bring their scripts to Shakespeare Club. I'm concerned a piece of dangling green wool might stigmatize them, but no, they're delighted to be singled out. I tie a knot around each tender wrist with a wink.

As I race off, I hear, "That's Ms. Ryane, the Shakespeare teacher. No you don't—you don't know her . . . only *some* of us know her!"

I like that I'm prized. They own me. I'm as cherished as a pet rock.

"Miles, did you bring your script?"

"I forgot."

"But the green wool on your wrist, what happened to that?"

"I took it off."

"Why?"

"I forgot what it was for."

Am I asking too much?

On the board:

A REAL ACTOR:
1. LISTENS TO THE DIRECTOR AND DOES AS SHE ASKS
2. NEVER TELLS ANOTHER ACTOR WHAT TO DO
3. HAS THE COURAGE TO BE SILLY
4. NEVER WHINES

"Okay, who read more of the play and can tell us what happens in the story?"

They glance at each other. Then at the floor. The ceiling, the door, the clock . . .

"Hermia and Lysander are in the forest and some men are in the forest because they're going to do a play and then Oberon and Titania have a fight and that's as far as I got."

"Anna, excellent. I'm impressed you read this on your own."

"Suck!" Hissed and vicious. I snap my eyes up.

"Who said that?" I stare them down, and they stare right back. "Does name-calling seem like 'helping and sharing'? You remember our mottos, right?"

They look at the floor.

"We say those mottos because we're supposed to mean them."

It pisses me off, this name-calling business. Anna looks humiliated, in part because I've singled her out. She shrinks as she toys with her fluffy pink boa. I'm not helping her, and I decide to drop it. A piece of green wool on a skinny wrist might not cause stigma, but doing the work and speaking up is risky business.

"For the rest of you who chose not to read the play at home, we're going to continue *A Midsummer Night's Dream* and find out what happens."

"I don't wanna be a boy. . . ."

"Stella, look at number four on the board." I point to the rules. "Never whines."

Stella frowns.

"You should take that rule personally."

Daniel is back today. He and Miles have created an overwhelming testosterone cocktail. They grab the markers and sprint to scribble on the board. I confiscate the markers. They fling themselves to the floor and roll and wrestle like bear cubs. I corral them and separate their seats. They slide them back together as soon as I turn away.

"Have you been robbed yet?" Marin asks.

Yet? Robbed yet? What is this, Oliver Twist?

"Pardon me?"

"You know, robbed . . . like from your purse or something."

"No," I swallow. "I have not been robbed, and I don't expect to be robbed." I scan the room for my purse. There it is, sitting alone on a shelf and wide open in a state of trust one could only describe as plain stupid. I slide my way over and zip it up.

"Why do you ask me that, Marin?"

She shrugs. "Sometimes it happens, that's all."

"Okay, let's say that's true, and let's also say that never happens in Shakespeare Club."

Marin nods but raises her eyebrows as if to say I'm living in a fool's paradise.

"Was this something you were thinking of doing?"

"No! I would never do that. Teachers always get robbed here, and I don't want you to, that's all."

Marin's warning me. Protecting me. She has street smarts and knows I don't.

"Thanks for the heads-up. Let's remember that here in Room 15, we don't call each other names and we don't rob each other." This gets a big laugh, but I'm unsure if my point is taken.

"Following Hermia into the forest are Demetrius and Hermia's best friend, Helena. Helena doesn't think she's as pretty or as adorable as Hermia. And Helena's in love with Demetrius. Poor Helena is at her wits' end. Demetrius and Lysander want Hermia, and no one wants Helena. Anyone here ever feel like that? Like Helena? She was lonely in a dark forest and thought no one loved her."

Every hand is raised.

"I'm going to give you two hot tips to battle loneliness."

On the board:

1. READ BOOKS

"If you read, you will always find characters to hang out with."

2. LEARN TO COOK

"If you learn to cook, you can always invite a stranger over for dinner and make a new friend."

"Ms. Ryane." Jennifer has her hand in the air. "We aren't allowed to talk to strangers. We can't invite them over for dinner!"

They're so damn literal.

"When you meet new people and get to know them *somewhat*, then you can invite them over and cook them something delicious."

"My mom says me cooking would be a disaster," Dana pipes up. "She says I'm too fat and I have one chin too many." Dana laughs, and a few others join in with her. I don't find this so funny.

"In the play, Puck says, 'Lord, what fools these mortals be!' What are mortals? Does anyone know?"

Anna's hand shoots up. "Is it like real people?"

"Yes. People are mortals. We are mortals. In *A Midsummer Night's Dream*, Shakespeare created people like us, and he had fairies. The King and Queen of the fairies and all the little fairies."

All the girls want to be fairies. In my adaptation, the fairies barely speak. Their main job is singing a lullaby to Titania, their queen. Nevertheless, the competition to be a fairy has begun.

"Meanwhile, in another part of the forest, six jolly men are rehearsing a play. These guys are buddies, and they're going to write and perform a play for the royal wedding that's to take place in four days. The kings and queens of that time would order up plays for weddings and celebrations."

As soon as I say *celebration*, I flash on Azra. I had cast her as a fairy, and like a fairy, she had flitted off. This is new to me, this teaching hazard. They leave you. They move on. And we're left with ghost children in our heads.

"Just think of me as Mrs. Spider," she said as she bent down to me. "My name is Mrs. Snider, but think *spider* and you'll always remember my name." She took my hand and led me into the first-grade classroom. She showed me her desk and found a desk for me. I slid into the seat and stuck my hands inside the wooden space for my stuff.

I was six and in school for the first time because I had never attended kindergarten. My mother reasoned that her kids would be in school a long time and should have another year to play. She also realized keeping her eldest at home would provide a babysitter for the younger two. I started first grade devoid of basic skills. I couldn't read, count, or name colors. I find this weird and disturbing.

"How many pennies do I have?"

"What color are the carrots?"

"What does the red sign mean?"

These are the basics of parent-child conversations. It was strange these interactions didn't occur between me and my mother, but they didn't.

The big school building with its steep stairway, porcelain-white drinking fountains, solid wood railings, and rushing bodies terrified me, but there she was at the top, waiting. Mrs. Spider/Snider, in a dark green paisley dress. The first kind person I ever met.

Now, years later, I want to rush to her and say, "I'm okay, Mrs. Snider. I remember you and will forever be moved by your kindness." But I do not know where Mrs. Snider is, or if she's even alive. I have become a ghost child to her.

"In the play, Titania and Oberon have terrible fights. Titania is raising a baby boy she's adopted, and Oberon wants that boy. He declares revenge and makes Titania fall in love with a donkey."

I lay my script on my lap and look at them. "Why do you think they have such battles?"

"He's very mean," Jennifer says.

"He's just . . . so angry," Jordan adds.

"But why?" I prod. "Why do you think Oberon is so angry? Sometimes you get so angry. Why is that?"

They twist in their chairs.

"Because girls are stupid!" Miles explodes.

"Yes, Miles, sometimes girls do seem stupid and, let's face it, sometimes boys are stupid. But why is Oberon being stupid?"

Miles shrugs.

"Titania has lots of fairies around her. All of her little fairies love her. Oberon has just one fairy, Puck. Maybe Oberon is jealous of Titania. Maybe he wishes he had as much love as Titania does. When Oberon is jealous, he gets mean and plays an awful trick on her."

"What are our parts, Ms. Ryane?" Dana asks.

"I'm going to figure that out for next week."

"I know what part I want. Do you want me to tell you?"

"That's okay, Dana."

I know what she wants too, but this isn't going to go her way. I have exactly two boys in the club for a play crowded with male characters. This is going to take some finessing.

"I want to be a faaaiiirrryyy."

Three guesses, first two don't count.

"Stella, number four is still your number. Take a look at the rules. I repeat: whining will get you nowhere with me." I get them to their journals. "I think we have lots to write about today. Meanness, name-calling, jealousy . . . tough stuff."

The kids start journaling.

"What do you want to write about, Miles?"

He turns away from me.

"How about imagining what it would be like to be Lysander? What would it be like to run off into the forest?"

He lays his head on the table. I lean in.

"You know, Lysander carries a sword."

He gives me a skeptical look.

"Really, he does." I stroll away, knowing his eyes are following me.

"I get a sword?" He's sitting up, bright and alert.

"When you do the work. You have to earn it."

He picks up his pencil. One small step, one big sword.

CHILDREN'S WRITES

Dear Diary,

My daughter better marry Demetrius. She better NOT marry Lysander. If she doesn't marry Demetrius she either marries him, become a nun, or get her head chopped off. I want her to marry Demetrius because he is rich and Lysander doesn't have not one penny.

Sincerely,

Egeus

LESSON PLAN

A sword in hand can help. Boys have trouble sitting still and tend to absorb more when they're on the go. They learn on their feet. Get 'em up.

"They're so excited about *A Midsummer Night's Dream*," a teacher says to me. "They really seem jazzed."

"The kids come in and ask for books about Queen Elizabeth and William

Shakespeare," the librarian tells me.

"Oh, when is the play? I want to see it. I want to be there!" another teacher enthuses.

"Honestly, I'm not so sure there'll be a play," I answer with a half-smile.

"Of course there will be," she says, shocked.

"You see, I don't want to pressure these kids into giving a performance. The Shakespeare Club is really . . ." I search for the words, ". . . well, it's really more like a book club. We meet once a week and explore the world and writings of William Shakespeare. We're not really into the *show* part of it."

She blinked. "Well, whenever you do it, I'll be there! I've heard these kids talking about it, and they love it!"

What kids? Who are these children she's talking about?

CHAPTER VII

CAST AWAY

We will meet, and there we may rehearse most
obscenely and courageously.
A Midsummer Night's Dream Act I, Scene II

Daniel isn't coming!" Jordan announces.

"What do you mean?"

"He says he quit. He isn't coming." Jordan's eyes are wide, awaiting my response. "He's out there, in after-school."

"After-school" takes place on the fields and in the classrooms, where play is organized and homework is overseen. They are real programs, unlike the phony-baloney cockamamie thing I've got going on in Room 15.

"You guys unpack and get your scripts out. I'll be right back."

I march, fuming. Today, I'd planned to announce casting. And now, after spending hours juggling eleven actors for twenty parts, Daniel is quitting? After I'd cast him and chatted with him regarding his sticking with the program?

I scan the grounds for his skinny frame. Children race across the field, climb monkey bars, kick soccer balls, and smash tetherballs, and I spot him. Like lasers, my eyes focus on him horsing around. He's having a gay old time, holding forth at a picnic table, surrounded by other kids. Daniel has the swagger of a Vegas comedian circa 1962. He looks to be spinning tales and cracking one-liners.

"Daniel?" I glare.

He ignores me and continues with whatever smartass story he has going. His rapt audience gives me a once-over.

"Daniel."

The after-school counselor looks up from her paperwork to check me out. Daniel finally chooses to face me with a defiant smirk.

"We need to talk," I say.

"Well, I'm not coming back."

He's blowing me off. He's *nine*.

"Daniel, you will come over here right now and talk to me."

"But I said I'm not coming back."

The counselor stands and appears ready to call security. I ignore her.

"Be that as it may, you will still come over here and talk to me."

The kids surrounding Daniel watch for his next move in this schoolyard version of *High Noon*. I glower. Seconds tick by. The two of us, hands poised on invisible holsters, are glued to each other.

Daniel ends the showdown by slithering off the picnic table and shuffling over to me. I crouch to his level.

"What happened? You told me you wanted to do Shakespeare Club, and I believed you. You were given a script, the casting has been set, and now . . . what?"

He won't look at me. He scuffs the toes of his Nike Airs into the dust.

"You'll be letting the others down. Are you aware of that?"

"I just don't want to do it."

I stand, take a breath, and fire the last shot. "Fine. You don't have to come back today, but don't ever, *ever* come back again."

And off I storm, instantly bereft and ashamed. Why did I say that? Why did I act like a nine year old instead of the adult I'm supposed to be? My head bubbles with arguments. He tried, and it wasn't for him. He's too disruptive anyway. Why does it matter so much? Because I failed, and I don't know why or how, and I don't know how to fix it. Maybe it wasn't gripping, entertaining fun. Maybe he felt incapable.

I can hear the commotion in Room 15 as I near the door. How do I do this? They're all over the room. The board is filled with pictures and nonsense writing. They're wrestling over the markers.

"Quiet!" It's like screaming underwater, like a dream where my mouth is open but no sound comes out. "Sit! Sit down! Sit down now!"

Some of them obey, but most are giddy, sweaty, and teetering over each other. They look drunk. The whole scene has a rollicking barroom feel, as if we were in the Wild West during the Gold Rush. *Holy shit, why am I here?*

"Miles, we're starting. Come out and participate, or you won't find out what part you're playing." Miles hides, and I refuse to search for him.

"Ms. Ryane, is Daniel coming back?" Dana bursts out.

"Inhale, big, big breath . . . fill your tummy with air and hold . . . hold . . . hold. No, Daniel isn't coming back. Exhale—"

Cheers explode and echo off the walls.

"It's better if he isn't here. He's too wild," Dana declares.

"Big, big breath in. Well, I'm disappointed he's leaving, but there's nothing we can do about it. Exhale and hold it . . . out, out, out. . . ."

On the board: *toy boat*.

"Try this ten times fast," I say, and I launch. "Toy boat, toy boat, toy boat . . ."

"You said 'tay bot,' Ms. Ryane!" Candace laughs. They all laugh. I'm laughable, no two ways about it.

And finally I, too, laugh. Really, what else is there to do? My head is thick with the hangover of a bad dream. Except it isn't a dream. Daniel quit. He's gone.

Miles crawls out of somewhere to see what's so funny.

"Nice to see you, Miles," I say, exhausted.

On the board: AN ACTOR'S JOB IS TO TELL THE STORY THE WRITER WROTE.

"That's what you're all going to do. You're going to tell the story William Shakespeare wrote. But first we have to find out what happens in this story. Then you'll write in your journals. After that, I'll tell you what parts you'll be playing."

I have to think fast about what to do with Demetrius because I had cast the two boys opposite each other as the suitors.

"So, when we left off, six jolly men were rehearsing a play in the forest. Shakespeare's introducing us to the idea of a play within a play. Do you get that?"

Not really; they're pretty foggy on that idea.

"The six jolly men are doing a play about two characters, Pyramus and Thisbe."

The kids really don't understand what I'm talking about.

"Okay, let's try this and you'll see what happens."

Together, we read the Pyramus and Thisbe play, which mirrors the story of *Romeo and Juliet*.

Miles throws his arm up, and I'm curious about his unexpected interest.

"Yes, Miles?"

"Ms. Ryane, on *The Simpsons*, I saw—on *The Simpsons*. . . ." Miles pants with excitement and has trouble getting the words out.

"Miles, slow down. Go on, tell us what you saw."

"Is this Shakespeare? I saw Bart, he was doing *Hamlet* . . . is that Shakespeare? And Homer was a ghost—is that Shakespeare?"

"Yes, Miles, that is definitely Shakespeare. Would you like me to tell you that story? It has a ghost and a murder."

Yes, yes, they want to hear that story.

"Hamlet's a teenager, and he's a prince. He lives in a castle far away in Denmark, a very cold country, but he goes to college in England. While he's away at school, his mom, Queen Gertrude, sends him a letter saying, 'Hamlet, you have to come home because your dad, the King, is dead.' *What the what?*, Hamlet thinks. He zips home on a ship in time for the funeral, and guess what? The next day, right after the funeral, his mom marries his Uncle Claudius, which means Uncle Claudius is the new king."

They're riveted.

"One night, Hamlet's best friend, Horatio, is with some guards at the top of the castle, and a ghost shows up."

As I regale this engrossed group of children, it's as if I were telling them a true story about one of their neighbors. I begin acting the play out for them, crossing this way and that on my stage, the carpet of the United States. It's sad, in a way, that my career has been reduced to this, but an audience is an audience.

"The ghost is—get this—Hamlet's dad. So, Horatio gets Hamlet to come up and see the ghost for himself. And Hamlet has a completely freaky conversation with his ghost dad where he finds out Uncle Claudius actually *murdered* Hamlet's dad so he could become king."

I trowel the word *murdered* on as thick as a bricklayer.

"Was his mom having an affair?" Dana whispers.

"Well, I'm not sure," I whisper back, "but I think she married too quickly after her husband's death. She probably couldn't stand the idea of being alone. Anyway, it's now up to Hamlet to seek revenge for his father. He has to kill his own uncle, and that's such a hard thing for him. He's just a teenager, after all."

"Does he do it?" Candace whispers.

"Yes, he does."

They're still and quiet.

"How about one day, we all watch the movie together?"

"Yes, yes, yes!" they screech.

"Ms. Ryane!"

"Yes, Miles?"

"The Simpsons went to England, and they were at a theater or something and—and there was this actor—and Lisa was excited and—and this actor was doing something—oh yeah— *Macbeth* . . . Ms. Ryane, is that Shakespeare?"

"Yes, Miles, that is Shakespeare."

Miles squirms, beaming. He's on the inside track of Shakespeare now. The Shakespeare Club, the Simpsons, and Miles have reached détente, and he's suddenly interested.

"*Macbeth* is also about murder and a desire for power," I say, "and many people think the play is cursed."

"What is 'cursed'?" Anna asks.

"In the theatre, there's a rule that no one can say 'Macbeth' anywhere other than onstage. There's a superstition that if you say 'Macbeth' out loud, terrible things will happen. That's a curse."

"What terrible things?" Marin asks.

"Well, there have been productions where somebody said 'Macbeth' backstage, and people got sick or died or fell off a ladder . . . things like that. But there's a way to break the curse if someone accidentally says it."

"What?" Jordan asks.

"The person who said 'Macbeth' must go outside, spin around three times, spit, beg to come back in, and then say a swear word."

"Whoa!" Candace exclaims.

"Yes, Candace, sometimes cussing is allowed. Sometimes it is legal and necessary."

Candace shakes her head vehemently from side to side.

In this moment, I find reason to hope. Their minds are tinkering away at stuff they wouldn't have known had we not all been in Room 15 together chewing away on William Shakespeare's stories. In this moment, it all seems possible.

On the board: IF I CAN DO SHAKESPEARE, I CAN DO ANYTHING.

They write that down in their journals.

"You see, Shakespeare wrote mountains for us to climb. To read and act and try to figure out. His work was so monumental that we can only try to do our best, but in doing that, we are stretching our minds further than we ever thought we could."

"Ms. Ryane?"

"Yes, Jennifer?"

"What is monu . . . monu . . . that thing you said?"

"*Monumental* means 'gigantic.' There are huge movie stars in this city, yet many of them cannot do Shakespeare. But here you are at Arden Street Elementary, doing Shakespeare. You are doing something monumental. That's pretty neat, don't you think?"

On this positive note, I figure it's time to announce casting.

One by one, I hand out pieces of paper:

CASTING

GRACE, *Puck*	REGINA, *Hermia*
MARIN, *Narrator/Egeus/Francis Flute*	MILES, *Lysander*
CANDACE, *Nick Bottom*	JENNIFER, *Helena*
JORDAN, *Peter Quince/Fairy*	CARLA, *Snug/Fairy*
DANA, *Theseus/Oberon/Robin Starveling*	STELLA, *Tom Snout/Fairy*
	ANNA, *Hippolyta/Titania*

A hush falls over the room . . . and then the hue and cry. In a flash, Room 15 is transformed from cohesion to another rowdy free-for-all.

"But Mary didn't wear glasses," my mother said.

I couldn't breathe, socked in the solar plexus by betrayal of the worst kind. I couldn't speak. I stared in disbelief at my mom. She couldn't mean this. It couldn't be true. My mother had just returned from the ladies' auxiliary meeting at church, and I'd stayed up well past my bedtime waiting. I paced and waited, waited and paced, for casting news of the part I would have in the Nativity play.

I knew, at seven years old, exactly how I would play Mary. Serious and solemn. I'd tenderly hold the baby Jesus and lay him to sleep in the straw bed. I'd give kind looks to the shepherds, but I wouldn't get too close to Joseph because he smelled a bit odd. I was ready to be Mary, dressed in long, pale robes. I wouldn't even be nervous, and I'd make my family proud.

"What?"

"You can't be Mary. I told the other ladies that Mary didn't wear glasses, and that's that."

"What?"

"You can be an angel. Now go to bed. What are you doing up this late?"

In my head, I screamed, *Whoever saw an angel wearing glasses?*

Casting. It's tough.

"Yay, yay!" Anna shouts. "I'm the fairy queen, Titania!"

"What? Tom *Snout*?" Stella sneers, and then clutches her stomach like she's been shot.

"Hermia . . . oh . . . I'm Hermia," Regina murmurs, and Stella looks ready to haul off and slug her.

"Nick Bottom?" Candace screams. I should have anticipated this reaction. "I'm a donkey? No!"

In Shakespeare's world, 'round the stage of ye olde Globe Theatre, these same cries of joy and devastation were heard. The casting of a play is either fabulous or horrible. Ah, the theatre and its vagaries of delight and heartbreak.

I rush the kids out the door and run to my car. I don't want to have these conversations. I don't want to argue and cajole. I gotta get out of here.

The one screaming omission from the cast is the role of Demetrius. With Daniel out, I'm left to solve the problem. There's simply no obvious answer, and I feel stuck. Daniel, Daniel, Daniel . . . it's a good part too.

CHILDREN'S WRITES

Dear Diary,
I don't want to be Hermia.

LESSON PLAN

Dump expectations and help them dump them, too. Expectations guarantee disappointment.

I open my car door and notice Dana on the street corner waiting for her mom to pick her up. Dana is a hulking figure with slumped shoulders. She shifts on one foot to the other in a portrait of desolation. Dana's efforts to fit in and be liked must be draining.

"Hey, Dana!" I call out, all chipper. I walk over and put my hand on her shoulder. "The roles of Theseus and Oberon are probably not the parts you wanted, but you have a great big voice, and I need an actor with that kind of presence to play those parts."

She nods, but her disappointment is obvious.

"I wanted to thank you ahead of time for taking these roles on. You're going to be really good."

"I gotta go, Ms. Ryane. There's my mom's car." She lumbers away. My pep talk hasn't made a dent. This is only one of the many disappointments Dana and I would share.

CHAPTER VIII

PROP ME UP

I long to hear the story of your life, which must
Take the ear strangely.

The Tempest Act V, Scene I

On the board:

GO TO SLEEP, CLOSE YOUR EYES,
TOMORROW'S A NEW DAY;
GO TO SLEEP, CLOSE YOUR EYES,
TOMORROW WE WILL PLAY.

The fairies' lullaby, the song they'll sing to Titania. I find a note, lift my hand, and sing while conducting the kids. Some sing right away, and others join in gradually. Miles has no intention of singing. His eyes roam the room in search of mischief. I move behind him and let my hand rest on his back. He squirms.

"Go to sleep, close your eyes . . ." Stella sings loudly, Grace softly.

Jordan sings with gusto, but Candace doesn't sing at all. She stares at the floor with pursed lips. The innocence of a lullaby undercut by the dark mood of a child's pain. I sing and wander behind their chairs, occasionally placing my hand on a back, a shoulder, a head. When I get to Candace, she wriggles away as if my touch burns her.

Carla sings at the top of her lungs. Opening her arms wide and throwing her head toward the ceiling, she mimics a grandiose opera singer. Grace laughs at Carla. The reaction sends Carla to even crazier heights. Dana uses her big voice; I hope that she's taking to heart our conversation from last week.

Go to sleep, close your eyes,
Tomorrow we will play.

Stella's cousin, Jennifer, silently mouths the words. Not everyone wants to stand out, and no one wants to be laughed at. To be mocked is to be touched with a hot brand that can scar. Many of us got those gibes—still get them—and they hurt.

Carla's figured out that clowning gives her the power to prevent anyone from laughing at her first. Miles has learned that by hiding, he can avoid classroom criticism. Marin struggles to balance good behavior with a desire to jab anyone who gets too close. Stella makes fun of others in order to protect herself. She plays in murky waters. Stella can and will become a mean girl.

Grace giggles at anyone who tries to make her laugh, and she has the talent to shrug off any attack that comes her way. She's rewarded by being left alone.

The children in Room 15 blush at even the tiniest of missteps.

I'm asking them to do a comedy. I'm asking girls to play boys' parts. I'm asking them to sing loud and use an archaic language. The one boy in our cast is being asked to play the part of a young man in love. They'll be on the frontline before an audience, and they're already fearful.

On a table: the Shakespeare Club box.

On the board: MAY 25.

"What do you think happens May 25?" I ask.

"The play?" shouts Stella.

"That's correct. That's the day we do the play. As we get closer to that date, I'll be checking in to see how you feel about doing it. To perform *A Midsummer Night's Dream* will be your decision."

Then I open the box and draw out props, one by one. The hush is broken with an occasional "oooh" or "awww" as they press forward to see.

I've spent hours twisting wire into fairy halos, covering each in silken ribbons of purple, pink, and yellow. I set these side by side on the table. A furry donkey mask for Nick Bottom's transformation comes next. Candace's face is a combination of curiosity and worry. I stroke the soft donkey ears, making sure she sees how valuable it is.

There's a lantern for the moon, crowns for Oberon and Titania, a blue flower for Puck's magic potion, and a scroll for Peter Quince's cast list. With a flourish, I extract two shiny, golden, plastic swords for Demetrius and Lysander.

Miles leaps out of his chair and grabs for one, but I hold it back.

"These are the props for our play, but I need to see disciplined rehearsals before they get used. When I see good work, a prop will be given to the appropriate actor. Is that fair?"

"NO!" they scream in unison.

"Wait a minute, don't you remember rule number one? 'Listen to your director and do as she asks'? Well, my young thespians, I'm the director, and I hold the cards on this one."

"Ms. Ryane?"

"Yes, Carla."

"You talk weird."

"This is true. Nevertheless, I still hold the cards."

"What cards?"

"*The* cards."

I show them a bag of highlighter pens and demonstrate how actors mark their lines in their scripts. They fight over the colors.

"I want pink!"

"Give me green!"

"Purple, purple!"

The battle escalates, and I grab back all the pens, raise my hand high, and wait. The racket subsides. "Let me see you take direction. Sit down at a table."

They do.

"I'll hand you a pen and you'll color in your lines, but you will not fight with each other."

And it happens.

"Marin, come with me."

I have a music stand in front of my chair, and I adjust it to her height. "Open your script to page one and set it on the stand. We're going to rehearse your narration."

Marin looks both surprised and delighted. She grabs her script and waits at attention for me to begin. But I'm distracted by Candace, at her desk with her head down on her script. She isn't writing, and she isn't highlighting. Is she sleeping?

"Just a second, Marin."

I kneel next to Candace. "Hey, is there a problem?"

She shrugs, but she won't lift her head.

"Why don't you choose a highlighter and color your lines?"

Nothing. She shifts in her chair, turning her body away from me. Candace shines me on and has no intention of doing anything I ask. Not today. Not going to happen.

"Candace, after we finish today, you and I will have a meeting."

I return to Marin. "Okay, Marin, give it a go."

She begins reading at warp speed.

"Yikes, just a sec. Marin, you're the glue keeping this play together. It's your narration that helps the audience understand the story."

She listens and nods. She's calm and attentive. I've never seen her like this.

"So you want to slow down . . . a lot. Speak clearly, and tell me the story as you read. It's like drawing pictures with the words."

She starts again, slightly slower. It's still far from where she needs to be, but I'm ecstatic. Marin took direction. She wants my undivided focus. In that moment, I get it. It's what they all want. It's what we all want: recognition and attention. I'm going to have to find the time to do this with each of these kids. It'll mean more than the current one-day-a-week commitment. I'll have to show up more days in order for a May 25 performance of any kind to occur.

Screaming and crashing chairs startle me from my work with Marin. An absolute breakdown is taking place behind me. I've turned away from them a little too long. Kids are at the whiteboard scribbling, others are gossiping behind cupped hands, and someone has opened the Shakespeare Club box.

"New rule," I announce. "No one but Ms. Ryane ever opens the Shakespeare Club box. Old rule: no one writes on the board! What the heck is going on here?"

A sword is missing. A boy named Miles is also missing. Patience itself is about to go missing. I glance at my pal, Mr. Clock. Thank God it's four.

"Okay, clean-up time. See you next week."

They drop everything, rush for backpacks, scurry to the door, and yell as they escape.

Candace still has her head on the desk.

"Okay, Candace, let's have a meeting."

Her sister Jordan lingers on the side of the room, as if holding up the wall. Her eyes, etched in suspicion, stay on me. She acts as her sister's guard, wary, as if Candace might be attacked.

"Jordan, wait for Candace outside. We'll just be a few minutes."

Jordan doesn't move.

"It's okay, Jordan, she's not in trouble. She's having a bad day, and we're going to talk about that."

I lead Jordan to the door, but it's not easy. She pulls away, hanging back, watching Candace.

"Jordan, come on . . . it won't be long, and nothing bad will happen, I promise."

She manages to move, ever so slowly, to the door. Outside in the sun, Jordan blinks as if shocked to find herself there.

"Why don't you sit on this bench?"

She sinks and clutches her backpack to her chest. I return to the room.

"Candace, come here."

Her hands are clasped on the desk with her forehead on top of them. I place two chairs in the center of the room. After a few minutes, she unfolds her body, shuffles across the room, and sinks into the chair across from me. Candace's head slumps toward her chest, tendrils of long brown hair falling forward. She will neither speak nor look at me.

We stay like this in Room 15, as long minutes tick by. Two fat teardrops trickle down her cheeks and fall on her clutched hands. Candace doesn't brush the tears away or acknowledge them in any way at all. *Drip, drip, drip . . .*

I rest my arms on my lap and lean in. I want to enfold her in my arms and erase whatever this is, but I don't want to scare her.

"'Candace, what is it? What's making you so sad or mad or whatever you're feeling?"

The tears turn into a stream. She doesn't speak.

"Candace, you can tell me anything. I'm on your side and I want to help you, but I can't if you don't tell me what's going on."

Nothing.

I place a tissue in her hands. It sits there for a full minute before her fingers toy with it. She squeezes it, crumples it, twists it, but she doesn't wipe her eyes. She looks tired. She looks middle-aged.

"Okay, I'm going to start a sentence and you fill in the end of it. Here we go. I feel . . ."

Nothing.

I try again, lifting my voice with encouragement. "I feel . . ."

Nothing.

"You can do this. Here we go: my name is Candace, and I feel . . . I feel . . . what?"

"Mad," she squeaks.

"I feel mad because . . ."

"They're . . . making fun of me . . . for being Nick Bottom."

"Candace, do you want to be in Shakespeare Club?"

"Yes," she whispers.

"Has anyone ever made fun of you before about . . . oh, anything?"

"No."

"Have you ever made fun of anyone else?"

"No."

"Sure you have. Everyone does that. That's part of what going to school is all about."

In desperation, I scuffed the horrid black Oxfords. Maybe the gray schoolyard dust would make them disappear altogether. My mom had a passion for making costumes and uniforms. When I was three, she dressed me as a nurse in a pressed white cotton pinafore emblazoned with a large red cross. To complete the outfit, she made a small pointy cap, also marked with a crimson cross. Every year until I was six, she'd whiz away on her Singer, sewing larger nurse's uniforms as I grew.

"It'll be your job to give sick people their shots, and you'll have to change their bedpans and take their temperatures."

Bedpans? What was she talking about? What sick people?

When I was old enough to join Brownies, and after that Girl Guides, my mom insisted on sewing my uniforms. Her obsession reached its pinnacle when she decided all schoolchildren should wear uniforms and "once and for all stop this faddish compulsion to be trendy."

"Oh, you look *smart*," she said. "Smart" was clipped and firm, and it meant "not up for discussion."

"Turn around," she said, smiling. "Let me see."

I made a slow twirl, and she gleamed at her handiwork. She caressed the pleats of the dark blue jumper with its matching belt. She folded down the collar of the white Oxford shirt and tugged up my navy knee socks. Then she licked a tissue and gave a final spit and polish to the black clunkers on my feet.

In this uniform, I was prepped and ready to attend a Catholic girls' school.

Problem was, I was actually going to a *public* school where children dress in

REGULAR clothes, *MOM!*

But this was not up for discussion.

I haven't seen or heard anyone making fun of Candace. This doesn't mean it hasn't happened; it only means I haven't seen it. But something, real or imagined, has happened to upset Candace this much. Being cast as Nick Bottom could have triggered something injurious from home, another class, or the playground. I don't know and I can't figure it out without hard evidence.

"Acting takes courage, Candace. Not everybody can do it. I cast you as Nick Bottom because I believe you're brave. If you crumble, they win."

"But they'll laugh at me."

"I hope so! That's what you want. Nick Bottom is the funniest part in the play. Actors all over the world want to play Nick Bottom because he's silly and makes the audience laugh."

She scowls.

"It's true. You have to trust me, Candace." I take both her hands in mine. "I'm not going to let you go out there and look like a fool. You'll learn some important stuff about yourself that'll help you be a brave girl forever. You can be the hero of this production."

I squeeze her fingers, hoping she'll believe me.

"Want to try?"

"What are you *wearing*?" asked Cindy, disgust vomiting from her mouth. She grabbed my shoulder and forced me to face her in my hideous school uniform. Her eyes went up and down and down and up, and I started to sweat.

I wrenched away from Cindy to continue my trek across the long stretch of playground. I knew without checking that I was being watched by my mother from our kitchen window, which was directly across the street from the school.

Do other kids want to knife their moms in the back? Does Cindy, with her perfect straight, blonde locks and zippy sneakers, fantasize about strangling the woman who dresses her every morning?

"Shoulders back. Never let them see you cry."

This was my mother's mantra. She fancied she'd buoyed my spirits with a shove toward the war zone armed with this useless homily.

Leaving Cindy behind, I could hear my mother's voice in my head. "Shoulders back. . . ."

When actors do well, we say we "killed." The audience was in our grip as we twisted and turned their emotions with the expertise of puppeteers. On that schoolyard, sucking up sobs with gritted teeth, I began my training to kill.

"No one laughs at *you*." Candace studies our joined hands.

"Sure they do. People laugh at me . . . I think my dog laughs at me. You want to give Nick Bottom a try?"

She shrugs and gives a small nod.

"Great. Next week, we'll figure out Nick Bottom." With a tattered tissue, I wipe Candace's eyes. "Come on, poor Jordan is worried sick about you."

I give Candace a hug, and we leave and bump smack into Jordan, who's pacing with the anxiety of a mother cat separated from her kittens.

"See you next week, girls."

Jordan and Candace exchange a silent look, and off they go, separate but equal, and a mystery to me. Is Jordan afraid of something I might say to Candace, or is Jordan afraid of something Candace might say to me?

I'm chilled in the warm sun. I don't believe this scene had anything to do with Nick Bottom.

Damn, damn, damn. We're never going to get this play up. Never ever.

I lean against the doorjamb as the twins lug their backpacks toward whatever home life awaits them. I want to cry, but I don't. Instead, I hum the lullaby: *go to sleep, close your eyes, tomorrow's a new day; go to sleep, close your eyes, tomorrow we will play. . . .*

Man, I need a nap, bad.

"When you go to school, you'll find out the truth, I'm telling you!" Judy screamed at me.

Judy was eight, and I was six. Judy was in the third grade, and I was about to start first.

"The man comes to the school in a big car and watches kids at recess. Then when he feels like it, he steals children and takes them away in his car."

I forced myself to laugh out loud at Judy. I pushed the laughs out of my stomach and aimed them at her, proving . . . proving—and tried hard to breathe at the same time. All the air in the world had disappeared, and I was suffocating. I hurried away from Judy, faster and faster up the gravel back lane. Have to get home, have to get home—but don't let big Judy see my face.

"He might not pick you!" Judy called after me. "But then again, he *might* . . . I just can't say!"

I climbed up the long back stairway of our house, where Mom was on the phone on the other side of the screen door. I rushed in, buried my face in her apron, and released terrified cries.

"Oh, honestly, Peg, I have to go. I have a little mess in front of me right now . . . some kind of tragedy, I'm sure. I'll call you later." Mom hung up.

"Judy Dilly said that?" she shouted after hearing my story. "She's a little liar, that girl. Do you actually think I would send you to a school where children are stolen? That Judy Dilly is an idiot. That whole family is nuts, for God's sake. Here, blow your nose and just forget her. Supper is soon . . . go now, get your brothers, and wash their hands. Honestly."

I washed my brothers' hands and managed to join my family at the table. Between bites, I wondered if this would the last meal I shared with them before being kidnapped on my first day of school.

My dad chewed on a chicken bone. I would miss him. My brothers opened their mouths to show each other half-eaten potatoes. I wouldn't miss them so much. My mother's face was stern. She knew what I was thinking and adamantly shook her head at me, maintaining our little secret. At times like these, my mom could be completely trusted. No one was taking me anywhere without her say-so.

CHILDREN'S WRITES

Dear Diary,

I want to tell you how life as being a fairy is. I get to sing lolabys to tatania the qween fairy. But one day the fairys and I sung a song to here. When she wouk up she fell in love with a monster. It was a donkey!

LESSON PLAN

No matter how much you want to rescue, no matter how much they need saving, you can only offer respite and power.

"Do you think I'm funny?" I ask William over dinner.

"No."

"Really?"

"Really."

"You're lying."

"Am I?"

"Yes, and I am funny, I will have you know. Many, many people think I'm an absolute riot."

"Do they?"

"The kids don't think I'm funny either."

"But what do they know?"

"I want a hug."

And I get a hug and a kiss and a gentle hand on my head. As William does this, I picture Titania, queen of the fairies, brushing the soft head of Nick Bottom, who has turned into a mournful donkey. And so this is love.

Tomorrow's a new day.

CHAPTER IX

A ROCK AND A VERY HARD PLACE

How shall I know if I do choose the right?
The Merchant of Venice Act II, Scene VII

On the board:

REHEARSAL!
FOCUS, LISTEN, DO.

I'm facing eleven empty chairs. We were thirteen, and now we are less. The space resonates with forest trills from the CD player. Despite Stella's disdain for these ambient sounds, I'm determined I can make an impression and find order in their chaos. As an experiment, I meditate. With closed eyes and deep breaths, I still my thoughts. Gentle birdcalls and breezy rustles wash over me.

My fantasy is rich. I imagine them arriving and seeing me like this. *Lead by example.* I picture the children, one by one, settling into their chairs to copy me. Together, we'll create an ashram of peace.

The school bell peals, and here they come, racing toward Room 15. I bite my lip to stop smiling. I'm certain, so very positive, my plan will work. They're descending with shrieks, and I know, in a matter of mere minutes, they'll want to impress me. Any second now, they'll be seated with closed eyes, and silence will reign . . . I suck in another deep breath and release . . . any second now—

"What's *this*? Ms. Ryane, what are you doing? This stuff again?" Stella's voice is the first to pierce the tranquility. "What's going on?" she demands, horribly shrill.

Eyes closed, I reach my arm up to waft her toward a seat. Others charge in, chattering about field trips and their red-hot Cheetos. I'm ignored. I tighten my jaw and blink my eyes open.

Here I am, in the center of the party, yet totally invisible. Why the *&%@#! do I plan these things? I leap up and get to work.

"Okay, let's begin."

They turn to me as if I just showed up.

"Oh, hi, Ms. Ryane," Marin says.

"Nice to see you. Please look at the board. We're officially starting rehearsal. Today. Right now. Ready?"

"Ms. Ryane," Jennifer asks, "who's playing Demetrius?"

I'd hoped to postpone that decision, but Demetrius shows up on the first page. *Think fast.*

"Stella, I'd like you to play Demetrius."

Maybe giving the girl more responsibility will end her dread whining—

"But I want to be a faaaiiirrryyy!"

I was mistaken.

"You can still be a fairy and Tom Snout, but you're a good reader and capable of playing Demetrius as well."

"Okay!" she chirps, accepting the compliment.

She opens her script. All ages are susceptible to flattery.

Off to the side of our horseshoe, Dana stares into space, tears running down her cheeks. She isn't sobbing or gulping, but those are definitely drops spilling off her chin. She bats at the flow with the back of her hand.

"Ms. Ryane," Candace pipes up. "Dana is crying."

"I see that. Dana, hang in, and we'll talk during the break."

Dana gives me a dramatic, slow nod. It's so portentous that my stomach clenches, and I wish I hadn't made the suggestion. This will be a can of worms, and I don't have an appetite for them.

Marin, at the music stand, has her eyes on me, like a musician ready to be conducted.

"Quiet, everyone, we're starting. Okay, Marin, take it away."

As she reads, Stella joins in, speaking along with her.

"Stella, no . . . this is Marin's part. She doesn't need help. You follow along in your script and pay attention to when one of your many parts comes up. That would be a good time to speak."

Stella giggles and screws up her face, acting cute. In Stella's world, whining and being adorable carry considerable cachet. Somehow, she's learned how to get away with murder by being girlish. She's slowly and deliberately driving me insane.

Marin begins again and slips up on *worthy*. She says "worry."

"Worthy, Marin, *worthy*," Jennifer corrects.

"Alright, let's take a good look at rule two: 'A real actor *never* tells another actor what to do.'"

"But Ms. Ryane, she said 'worry,' not 'worthy,'" Jennifer protests.

"I know you think you're helping, but you're not. This rule will be the toughest for all of you, but it must be obeyed. Only the director can tell an actor what to do. You have to pay attention to your own work."

I scan the room. They're listening. A good sign, so I continue.

"For example, is anyone here ready to read the chorus? It's coming up and *chorus* means all of you."

A couple of them peruse their scripts. Miles eyes the door.

"Marin, please, again."

She stumbles her way through the opening speech.

I take Dana's hand, lead her to the center of the carpet, and gesture for her to speak. She starts small but gains momentum and volume.

DUKE THESEUS
*Either to die the death, or to abjure
Forever the society of men.*

Her Duke Theseus, for no good reason, is weeping, but I pretend all is well in our imagined Athens.

"That's terrific, Dana. Good attack on the speech."

Regina joins sniveling Dana at center stage and freezes, quite dismayed. Her script is open to Hermia's lines, but her true love, Lysander, is crouched underneath his chair.

I focus my attention on Regina, Dana, and Marin. Marin has to leap away from her music stand and onto center stage for her role as Egeus. A lightning transformation from one character to another would be nothing less than a miracle for a seasoned actor, let alone a rank nine-year-old, but I have faith.

As more characters step into the scene, a child-huddle begins to form. They face each other in a tight group, scripts held high.

"Kids, the audience needs to see your faces. You have to spread out and cheat your bodies to the front."

"Cheat? Cheating isn't allowed," Regina admonishes.

"That's what it's called in the theatre . . . cheating your body outward so we can see you."

"But we don't want you to see us," Regina answers.

"I know it's scary, but please start doing this now. It'll feel very powerful when you're in front of an audience, and they can understand the story by seeing you."

"Ms. Ryane, when's our break?"

We're exactly two pages into rehearsal.

I get them settled with a snack of carrots and ranch dip, and I lead Dana to a corner. She slurps up a big sniff.

"Dana, what's going on?"

"Mr. Davis kicked me out of chorus and student council. My mom is going to kill me when she finds out. She'll take away my camcorder and ground me forever," she erupts, one sentence toppling over another. "And I didn't do it, I *didn't*."

"Didn't do what, Dana?"

"He said I hit someone, a little kid, and I didn't . . . I really *didn't*."

"Well, I wasn't there, so I don't know what really happened—"

"I *didn't*, Ms. Ryane!"

It's difficult not to believe her. "If I were you, I would go to Mr. Davis and tell him you think there may have been a misunderstanding and that you'd like another chance. Ask him what it would take from *you* to make this happen."

She agrees to the plan, accepts a tissue, blows her nose, and heads for the carrots and dip. She turns back to me.

"I really *didn't*, Ms. Ryane."

"Okay."

I'm left wondering.

"Okay, everyone, break's over. Let's move on to page three."

Page three. This is how the Russians rehearse a play. They take years.

Regina, in place as Hermia, waits for her Lysander. Miles has curled up under a desk. Regina reads her lines in as big a voice as she can muster.

HERMIA
So will I grow, so live, so die, my lord.

Stella and Grace arrive, reading the chorus. The other kids continue to munch carrots.

CHORUS
Hermia was given three choices: marry Demetrius, become a nun, or die. It's up to Lysander to fix this problem.

We wait. We all wait. The kids watch me. I stare at the ceiling and scratch my throat, trying to figure out what to do.

"Miles, check out rule one: 'Listen to your director and do as she asks.' You're the actor and I'm the director, and I'm asking you to come out from under the desk and play Lysander. Take your place next to Hermia."

We wait. We all wait.

Miles snakes on his belly across the colored carpet, laboriously gets to his knees, and shuffles into place. His script hangs limp by his side, and he stares at the floor and refuses to look at Regina.

"Go ahead, it's your line," I say.

"How. Now. Why. Is. Your. Cheek. So. Pale. How. Chance. The. Roses."

"Miles, look again. You missed a bit—"

"No, no way! This is *nasty*! I'm not saying that! I'm not saying that word!"

He glares at me. Talk about your high drama. But I refuse to react. He bores into me. I match his challenge with a steady glower and give him ten seconds.

"Remember: 'We honor the works of William Shakespeare'? That's one of our mottos, Miles. Say your line. 'How now, my love' . . . go on."

Thud. He drops to the floor like a sack of bricks.

I close my script and cross my arms.

Miles is on the floor, eyes shut.

Regina, stunned, grips her script.

Dana rocks from one foot to the other.

Marin has crawled onto a table, where she lies staring at the ceiling.

Carla and Grace giggle, heads touching.

Jennifer and Candace have decided to hate each other and drag their chairs apart.

Jordan, in her own world, doodles in her script.

Stella and Anna study me.

"We will *never, ever* get this together. We are on page *three* of a *twenty-three-* page script," I wail.

No one moves. They have no idea why I'm upset.

"Everyone, go to your journals and write about today's work. Write about your first rehearsal. Miles, outside. *Now.*"

He drags himself up as if doing me a huge favor, and we step out the door into the sun. We sit across from each other at a picnic table.

"Miles, what is the problem?"

He shrugs.

"That's not an answer. I'm going to tell you exactly what I told Daniel. Shakespeare Club is not a class. You don't get grades, and you don't have to be here. Do you *want* to be in Shakespeare Club?"

"I don't know."

"Well, you have to know. I'm giving you the choice, today, right here, right now. You have to decide: in or out?"

"I don't know."

"Miles, life is choices. The choice you're making is to act crazy in the club. I'm giving you another choice . . . to leave it."

He plays with his fingers.

"Maybe this isn't right for you. It doesn't make you a bad person to leave. You don't have to do this."

He blinks.

"Do you want me to fire you? I could do that. Just fire you from the club."

"It's my parents!" he bursts out.

"What do you mean? Your parents are *making* you do Shakespeare Club?"

"They say I have to do this or be with my brother, and I don't want to be with my brother!" He's near tears.

"I see."

And I did see, because I'd noticed Miles's hulking older brother come by to pick him up. He's a good foot and a half taller than Miles. He may be a peaceful soul, but he has the look of a bully.

"Miles, my friend, you are what we call between a rock and a hard place. Do you know what that means?"

He shakes his head. I scavenge for a couple of small pebbles and a stick. I place the pebbles on the table and the skinny stick tight between the two.

"The stick is you. One rock is Shakespeare Club, and one rock is your brother. You're being squeezed from both sides, and it's unpleasant. Miles, this isn't the *only* time this will happen in your life. This is just the *first* time."

We stare at each other. He gets that I understand his predicament.

At nineteen years of age and three thousand miles away from home, I'd been cast as the ingénue in an obscure English comedy. I was the only female in the play, and I was in way over my head. I was surrounded by experienced male actors, and no one noticed my floundering.

"Help me, help me!" I cried in a tiny voice inside my head.

The director, a sputtering fellow with decades of work behind him, leaned backwards in his chair, reading a newspaper.

"When you do something interesting, I'll watch," he announced, snapping a page. The rehearsal hall echoed with snorts from the male actors. I was in a room full of people, but I felt entirely alone. I had to act like I knew what I was doing. "Shoulders back . . ."

I'd been hired by a celebrated theatre festival in a quaint Canadian town. The company had constructed a brand-new, 865-seat theater. To commemorate its opening, a slew of dignitaries would attend the theater over the course of the summer. Among them: the Queen of England, the Prime Minister of Canada, and Indira Gandhi.

Alongside the world's best and brightest would be 160 theatre critics on opening night.

I had no business being on that giant stage, and those scribes would say so—over and over and over. I'd read them and want to die.

The only time the director spoke to me directly was after the *second* night's performance. That morning, I'd seen reviews scattered across the kitchen table in the house I was sharing with other actors. I blanched as I read: *She's beautiful until she opens her mouth.*

For our second performance, my voice was barely above a whisper.

Those reviews were only some of the many horrible notices that would come to the attention of my young and lost self.

"You will never, do you hear me, *never* do that again—walk through a performance like a dead person—never again . . . I do not care what you read or think—you are a professional—now act like one!" the director screamed at me that day in a parking lot.

"But I don't know how," answered the small voice inside my head. "I don't know how to walk back out there. Help me, help me!"

My mother's reprimand came from far away. "Shoulders back . . ."

I finished my first professional summer as an actor. I searched for help, but I couldn't find any; yet, in crazy fortune, I kept being hired. I continued to struggle on large stages until I found a book that would change everything: *Respect for Acting.*

The book was practical and clear, and a lifeline. I wrote a letter to its author and begged for help.

"I'm a working actor. I'm being employed, but I don't know what I'm doing. Please help me."

And she did. One of the illustrious lights of the Broadway stage, Uta Hagen, heard my cry, let me audition for her acting class, and took me under her wing in order to help me sprout those of my own. She unzipped me, opened me up, and impressed upon me the notion that all artists have an obligation to bring their personal selves to their work.

"It is the very uniqueness of you and your life experience that makes an audience sit up and pay attention," she instructed.

This was both an alarming and freeing concept. Up to that point, I was doing little more than mimicking actors I admired. Uta Hagen was the first person to tell me *I* was of value. It was time for me to make the necessary and courageous leap of revealing myself in the character.

And I did.

Forever, I will thank her. She taught me how to fly.

"Look!" she'd cry to the class. "This is how we want to see Shakespeare done! That's it!"

She was pointing at me.

Uta Hagen became the mother to my craft. I found my voice under her tutelage.

"Unfortunately, Miles, you need to make a choice today, right this minute. I promise, if you stay with Shakespeare Club, you'll have a good time, but you have to commit, and you have to promise to behave. What's it going to be?"

He nods a little.

"Out loud. I need you to say it out loud."

Miles's declaration of this commitment appears outside the realm of possibility, so I take what I can get.

"Okay," he mumbles.

We reenter Room 15, and I address the group. "Miles has made a decision."

"He's quitting?" they shout.

"No. I'm happy to announce that Miles has decided to stay in the Shakespeare Club with renewed commitment, and he'll rehearse properly from now on."

I check with Miles for confirmation. His head has dropped, and I place my hand on his shoulder.

"Anything you want to say to the group?"

He shakes his head.

"Did I just speak the truth?"

He looks around at all the girls watching him.

"Miles, they have to know you mean it."

He tilts his head to me and gives the barest of nods. This will have to do.

"Okay, he's in, and that's it for today. See you next week."

When Uta Hagen died, a huge community of actors mourned her passing.

I saw that director again, the one who read a newspaper while I stumbled in rehearsal. He was no longer directing but had found work acting onstage. As I watched him, it became clear he had no idea what an actor does. He was old and still sputtering. He never could have helped me. He didn't know how.

I silently wished him a lovely afternoon, perhaps reading a newspaper on a porch. Those were the only boards on which he belonged.

CHILDREN'S WRITES

Dear Diary,

I am very mad that Lysander ran off with my wife, Hermia. I am so glad that Helena told me about their little scheme. But I don't have time to thank her because I have to stop what they are doing and the wedding . . .

Sincerely,

Demetrius

LESSON PLAN

There is never one truth. We're in a gray area, and we're in it together. Stuff happens, stuff is thought to have happened, and other stuff
will happen. You have to guess, reach for possibilities, and offer
choices.

That night, I tuck into bed next to William.

"I have to wonder why you would marry someone so humorless."

He mutes the game on TV. "I didn't say you were humorless."

"Yes, you did."

He puts his arm around me and kisses me on the cheek. "I said you weren't funny. But you have a great sense of humor."

"I don't believe that. Why would you want to marry someone who isn't funny?"

"I'm funny enough for the both of us, and you have the good humor to see that."

"I don't know who said you were funny."

"You did."

"Quiet, I'm sleeping."

CHAPTER X

MILES TO GO

... Banishment!
It comes not ill; I hate not to be banish'd,
It is a cause worthy my spleen and fury ...

Timon of Athens Act III, Scene V

In they scurry, Cheeto hands and all.

"Ms. Ryane, Ms. Ryane!" Grace shouts, throwing down her backpack.

"Yes?"

She runs over, followed by Carla, Stella, Jordan, and Jennifer. The girls form a circle around me, their faces bright with excitement. It's clear they're full of *news*. And I have an inkling it's not good news.

"Guess what?" Stella yells, as if I'm not directly in front of her.

"Regina quit!" Grace tops Stella.

I knew it. I knew the news wouldn't be good. *Dammit to hell*, but I don't say that out loud.

What is it with quitting? Is it easy? Because right now, I'd like to follow in Regina's footsteps.

Where I grew up, shame walked hand in hand with quitting. In Canada, we don't quit. We also never jaywalk and are unnervingly punctual. Invite a Canadian to dinner, and you'll be caught in the shower when the doorbell rings. We're like that.

I squeak out a low moan and twirl a strand of my hair, ready to yank it right out.

And the vultures descend.

"Can I be Hermia?"

"Please, please . . . let me be Hermia!"

"No, *me*! *Me*!"

Regina's absence means little more than an available role. And it's a great part. A girl part. The Holy Grail of girl parts in Room 15.

Last week, Miles abandoned his leading lady on center stage when he refused to say *love*. How humiliating this must have been for eight-year-old Regina. I was so busy wrestling with Miles, I hadn't paid Regina any attention, and now she's gone.

"Take your seats," I sigh to the hungry mob. "No one is going to be Hermia today. We're going to work with our six jolly men. We don't need a Hermia today."

They make a big fuss with loud groans, running in circles, dumping backpacks, and fighting over Cheetos and sunflower seeds.

Miles arrives last. One of his hands is clad in a fine set of cardboard Freddy Krueger nails. Each of his five fingers is now six inches long. He grins, proud of his accessory.

I rest my head in my hand. What does he expect me to say, or do, or think? Am I supposed to be impressed? Miles is tossing dry twigs on my fire. He's feeding my surly mood.

"Take a deep breath in, hold it . . . hold it . . . and exhale, squeeze it out . . . out. Eyes closed, Stella. And in, in . . ."

Pacing behind their chairs, I arrive at Miles, bend, and whisper, "Take them off and put them away, please." The *please* is long and less than friendly.

"Awww—"

"I know life is hard, but this argument is over. Deep breath in. Marin, eyes closed. Closed as in shut, Marin. Hold it . . . hold it. . . ."

Miles neither does the breathing nor removes the nails. Instead, he admires them like new Lee Press-ons, hand held high, turning it one way and twisting his wrist for another angle. Then he takes one long finger and scoops the purple flower prop from underneath Grace's chair. The plastic flower hangs in the air, dangling off one pointy digit, and Miles, with a flick, sends it flying across the room.

"Miles, take those off *right now*. Put them away and get Grace's prop back," I explode. Curse words tumble around in my head like balls in a bingo cage. I'm so, so close to screaming them out loud.

Miles slumps off and removes the Freddys before crawling on the floor and retrieving the lost flower. No one is more attached to slithering than Miles.

Apparently, I have to introduce another rule. "Never *ever* touch another actor's props."

"What's a prop?" Jennifer asks.

"Puck has a blue flower; that's Grace's prop. Oberon has a crown, Robin Starveling has a lantern . . . someone has a sword and so on."

I point out the props I've set under their chairs. They dive under and pull out a scroll, a handkerchief, a fairy wreath, and a donkey mask.

Under Miles's chair, there is nothing. He tips over and looks between his legs for something, anything. Down on all fours, he continues the search before shooting me a plaintive look.

"Miles, you have to earn the sword. When you really try with Lysander, you'll get the sword. Simple. Choices, remember?"

He dons a sullen pout and slouches with his arms crossed over his chest.

"I need six jolly men up onstage, please," I call out.

Candace leaps up as Nick Bottom, and Jordan joins her as Peter Quince. Stella, on all fours, gets in place as Snug, Marin is Francis Flute, Carla is Tom Snout and . . . and . . . where is Dana?

"Has anyone seen Dana? She's Robin Starveling."

"Oh, Ms. Ryane, Ms. Ryane!" Jennifer's hand springs up with another news bulletin. "Dana's sister had a baby yesterday, so Dana had to go straight home after school because now she's an auntie."

Oh boy. I really don't want to know the details about this one. How young is her sister and why is she having a baby and why is Dana an auntie?

"Ready, Marin? Go."

"A group of Athens's working folks gathered together to rehearse a perfor-mance for the Duke's wedding day . . . " Marin gets the narration out and jumps into her role as Francis Flute.

Nuts. This show will be nuts, no two ways about it.

In the play, Peter Quince, the director, announces casting. As he does, Nick Bottom, a ham of an actor, clamors to play all the parts. Bottom orates on how brilliant he would be in everyone else's role. Quince, frustrated, reminds Bottom that he has one part, and it is the only part he will be playing.

I identify with Peter Quince. The poor man writes a play, gathers together a raggle-taggle group of wannabe actors, and cannot get them to act. I could weep for Peter Quince and his headaches.

"What is Pyramus? A lover, or a tyrant?" Candace, as Bottom, asks.

Jordan answers, "A lover that kills himself, most gallant, for love."

"That will ask some tears in the true performing of it," Candace cries. "I will move storms!" She clutches her hands to her breast as she says this.

Candace's take on the character of Bottom is a riot. She's bold and bright. She uses a big voice and revels in the laughter coming from those of us watching. Everyone finds Bottom funny. Candace blushes and acts even bigger, stretching her arms wide and twirling around the other characters kneeling at her feet.

"Let me play Thisbe too! I'll speak in a monstrous little voice, 'Ah, Pyramus, my lover dear!'" she sings in a falsetto.

An actor at work, she feeds off our reactions. Wanting more, she throws herself onto the stage in a fashion every actor from the beginning of time would understand. This is a long way from the morose Candace of weeks previous. This is an actor riding high.

Jordan, as Quince, marches over, and Candace falls to her feet. Jordan towers over Candace, and real sister-to-sister conflict erupts hilariously, one battling the other as Quince and Bottom go at it.

"I will roar you as gently as a dove; I will roar you as 'twere any nightingale," Candace cries.

"You will play no part but Pyramus!" Jordan tops her.

Meanwhile, off stage right, Miles has reapplied his Freddy fingers. He's diabolical, this kid. I'd momentarily snapped out of grouchiness, and he's dragged me back. He wanders behind Jennifer and bats at her hair with them.

"Ms. Ryane!" Jennifer calls out. "Miles is bugging me! Ms. Ryane, please tell him to stop!"

I'm on my feet. "What are you doing?"

He strolls back to his seat. The others watch to see what I'll do, and I have to do something. It's not fair to the kids who want to rehearse to have Freddy Krueger in the room.

"Miles, come with me. The rest of you look through your scripts, and we'll start back up in a minute."

He follows me to the corner where the backpacks are piled.

"Is that yours?" I point to a blue backpack. He nods.

"Good, pick it up and follow me."

I open the door and usher him outside. He looks up, confused.

"You're fired. We had an agreement, and you broke it. So . . . you're fired."

I'm in between a scream and a sob. "I need Miles to play Lysander, not Bart Simpson or Freddy Krueger."

He squints at me in the sunlight, looking like he wants to say something, but he doesn't.

"Either go find your brother in the schoolyard or sit on that bench until he finds you."

He stares at the empty slab of concrete bench.

"We gave it our best crack, Miles, but I don't think Shakespeare Club is for you. I wish you very, very well. Goodbye."

His backpack slides off of his shoulder and falls to the ground. I close the door.

I'm acting harsh, but I'm sad. As breakup scenes go, this ranks pretty high for me in terms of surprise and drama. It isn't easy, this quitting/firing business. My gut clenches. Doubt and dismay flood me, but I can't torture the earnest members of the club with Miles's disregard.

My head spins as I return to their shocked faces.

"Okay then, where were we?" *Where indeed, Ms. Ryane?*

According to my script, we're on page four of twenty-three, and we're about to begin spring break. We're precisely nowhere.

On the board: MAY 25.

I face this group of eight (formerly eleven, formerly thirteen) actors attempting to do a Shakespearean play with twenty-two characters.

"That is the day we perform *A Midsummer Night's Dream* if we can get it together. What do you think?"

"We could do it." Jennifer widens her eyes, trying to inspire me.

"Please, Ms. Ryane, we can do the play . . . really, we can," Anna says.

This is something else I've learned: children have trouble grasping the concept of time. I can tell them we have five minutes, five hours, or five months, and they don't get the difference. After all, they think I know Shakespeare. Time is meaningless—to them. I know about time. How can we get to May 25 with a two-week break coming up and our rehearsals disintegrating every time we meet?

I signal to Marin to resume narrating.

"Lysander and Hermia ventured to the woods. Peter Quince and his actors also met in the woods. But none of them knew that this forest was home to a Fairyland . . ."

We're in a fairyland, alright. I glance at the clock in defeat. My casting deci-sions have gone out the window. I can't imagine how to do this or what the hell I'd imagined in the first place.

Lost in blue thoughts, I'm jolted back by Stella's voice.

"Ms. Ryane, what's Miles doing?"

The girls are out of their chairs and craning their necks to the windows.

Miles is peering inside between the narrow slats of the blinds. He ducks up and down to see us. He looks like Tiny Tim bobbing around, trying to get a look at what he's missing. He can't see us watching him. He looks so small. I feel like scum.

It doesn't matter if they like you, my sister-in-law's voice rings in my head.

How can it not matter? How can I stop that from mattering?

I think about the two pebbles and the little stick I'd used to illustrate being caught between a rock and a hard place to Miles. I feel like a small twig myself.

I force myself away from the window and rejoin the group.

"Miles made a choice, and we have to respect his choice. He didn't want to do the work and . . . you know . . . that's that. Now, we have fifteen minutes for journal writing."

I go to the windows and twist the blinds closed. Do I look as icy as I feel?

I could smell the cloakroom. The word tipped me to another time. Cloakroom? Why was it called that and not *coatroom,* for instance? As if we went to school wearing cloaks and leather gloves, having arrived by horse and carriage. It con-jured a Brontë novel, not the plain box of a boring, suburban elementary school.

"Into the cloakroom right now, Miss!" was a phrase directed to me on more occasions than I can number. It was the "bad kid" place. Punishment for being "mouthy," a "chatterbox," or a "crowd-pleaser."

Stuffed onto a hard wooden bench between wet jackets, scattered rubber boots, and errant damp mittens, I was instructed to "give some thought" to my actions. I didn't.

I liked the cloakroom. Out there, the teacher's chalk scratched and tapped words on the board, and I was relieved to be alone back here in exile. I didn't think about the crimes that had landed me here. *Fine with me, no problem. You all bug me anyway.*

Shutting Miles out makes me wonder if it's "fine" with him. Do we all bug him anyway? I want to crawl inside his head and know what he's thinking and what he needs. I want to fix this, but I don't know how. I recognize the isolation he's experiencing on that bench. Exile.

"Happy spring break!" I call out at four o'clock, the words catching in my throat.

Outside, Miles heaves his backpack over his shoulder and shambles away with the rest of them.

Miles, I'm sorry. I didn't mean it, please come back . . . I want to grab him and hold him. But I don't. That would be a mistake. Miles and I both have to reckon with our choices.

The kids' raucous laughter fades away as they scuttle off and leave me to the chore of cleaning up. Every chair feels like it weighs a hundred pounds. Every scrap of paper burns in my hand as I scrunch and toss it in the trash. I suck back tears, and my cheeks flare in shame.

CHILDREN'S WRITES

Dairy
  I thank courage is: to have guts.

LESSON PLAN

Learn to improvise. There is benefit to boundaries. There is advantage to follow-through. Yes, I have to say what I mean and mean what I say but . . .

We're human beings, grown and growing. There is much to be gained in bending. Like a willow to the earth, learn to bend.

"You can always quit."

My head is on William's shoulder.

"You taught them a lot, but maybe they're not ready for Shakespeare. Spring break may be the perfect time to end it. Time to walk away knowing you did your best."

I can't. I'll feel worse if I quit. I have to figure this out. I'm balanced precariously on a giant learning curve. They're also on a curve. The difference is that I know it and they don't. Learning curves are hard and they hurt. And I'm too damn Canadian to split.

I find Miles at a cafeteria lunch table. He's kneeling on one leg on the bench, crowded in by fellow fourth graders. They snort and spit their food with all the charm of nine-year-old boys.

I crouch behind him and place my hand on his sapling of a back. He stiffens and turns very slightly to see me out of the corner of his eye, like a nervous colt. In his hand, a crummy square of public school pizza. I'm at school the day before spring break in search of something with Miles. Unsure of what . . . forgiveness, or a clean break.

"Miles, I have your journal and your script here. You get to keep these."

There's no place on the crowded bench for me to set them. "Miles, lift your bottom, and I'll tuck these under you. You can put them in your backpack after lunch."

His only adjustment is to turn away from me.

"Are you his mom?"

"Is he in trouble?"

"What did Miles do?" The other boys are eager for information.

"I'm not his mom. I run the Shakespeare Club. Miles isn't in trouble."

"But what happened? What did he do?"

"This is kind of private between me and Miles, okay?"

They return to blowing pizza mush at each other.

I whisper to Miles, "Just lift a little, come on . . . up." I try to pry him up a tiny bit. It isn't working.

"Gosh, you don't want these to get lost. You really do get to take them with you." My resolution is weakening with the timbre of my voice. I sit back on my heels, uncertain of what to do next. My hand on his back is the only link between us.

Miles drops his chin to his chest, and balloon-like tears drip down his cheeks.

"Can I come back?" he whispers.

I take a breath. I have a nine-year-old boy in the palm of my hand. Could I possibly snap his future with a false move?

"You know, Miles, I don't think so. We've been through this a couple of times already. You and I made a deal, and you broke the deal. Maybe we'll do Shakespeare Club again next year . . . maybe you'll be a little more ready for it then."

He doesn't sniff. He doesn't wipe. He's very still, and the tears keep falling.

"Can I please come back?" The *please* doesn't warrant special emphasis. Every word of the question is delivered in the same even tone, making it all the more heartbreaking.

I bite my lip to buy some time.

"Okay . . . look, one last try."

My stomach tightens as I say this. Am I making a mistake?

But Miles has no reaction to my decision. No cheer, no yelp, no indication at all of him winning this small war. We are fixed in a hushed peace.

"But Miles, you have to stop hiding under the desks and talking when others are reading. You must stop stealing the other kids' props, and you really have to read Lysander like it's written. You can't just refuse to read it. Can you do all that?"

He nods, but he still won't look at me.

I move in to give him a hug because . . . really, I could've used a hug myself, but he isn't going to let that happen. My hand continues to rest on his back.

"I'm going to take my hand off of your back. I'm going to leave now, and you're going to finish your pizza. I'll keep your journal and script for you. I'll see you in Shakespeare Club after spring break."

I try not to look back. I don't want to embarrass him in front of his buddies.

But I'm curious, and as I glance back, I'm tackled by Grace, Stella, and Carla. They throw their arms around my thighs. "Hi, Ms. Ryane!"

"Hey girls, are you looking forward to spring break?"

"Nooo, we'll miss Shakespeare Club!"

"We don't want a break!"

What the hell is this? I feel myself tip into crazy as I try to realign the skewed realities of our experiences. We all want to be in Shakespeare Club. We all want to quit Shakespeare Club.

One more meeting in two weeks, and I could break up with them then. Yeah, that would be the plan, and it's a good one, too. I peel myself away from the gaggle of girls and grab a last look at Miles.

I'm surprised to see him watching me. I lift a hand in farewell, and he turns away to finish his cold pizza.

Yeah. That would be the plan. And a good one, too.

An argument has been put forth by some educators that our school system is becoming too feminized. In other words, in an effort to compensate for the quietness of the female student, we are ignoring and often punishing the challenging male student with a quick diagnosis of "disruptive behavior" and sometimes sloughing them off into special-ed classrooms.

The problem can escalate when the teacher is female and has no male offspring. As women, we like order, peace, obedience, and compliance.

Girls, when given an assignment, almost always settle in to complete it and await the reward of recognition. Boys want to know why, how, when. If they don't get an answer or have to wait their turn, they become unsettled and restless.

Miles is now the bravest boy in the whole school because he is the only boy in Shakespeare Club. He's struggling to comprehend a language and story completely foreign to him. He's suffering the slings and arrows of schoolgirls dismissing him and their outright meanness. And here I am, a woman, running the whole shebang.

Most startling is that he wants back in.

INTERMISSION

No more be griev'd at that which thou hast done:
Roses have thorns, and silver fountains mud,
Clouds and eclipses stain both moon and sun,
And loathsome canker lives in sweetest bud.

Sonnet 35

Brown cinnamon is sprinkled upon the foamy milk awaiting my sip. I can do little but stare at it. Lethargy, thick and gelatinous, has me in its grip. I methodically stir my coffee and wait for my thirst to appear.

A gas fireplace flickers with cozy flames. Velvety armchairs set the picture. A home away from home for these people, who click away on keyboards, get chummy with friends, and flip through newspapers. They look for distractions from a beckoning clock. They are grateful for a caffeinated escape. Soon they'll be back where they belong, necessary and needed. I am envious of these strangers.

William goes to work, where he is creative and indispensable. I'm envious of him, too. At this Starbucks, I can barely lift a latte to my lips. I'm lost.

I used to spend my days buzzing from one audition to another. Studying scripts, choosing the right clothes, and waiting for the phone to ring with a call time for rehearsal, for the set, for a meeting, for another audition . . . until . . . it all . . . started to creak . . . to a ponderous . . . stagnant . . . end.

The roles slipped from "guest star" to "featured." The thrill of playing a part switched to relief at booking the part then to the sadness of having to show up and play "second doctor from the right." In the theatre, I was even more miserable. I grew tired of another city, another show, and not having a home with roots.

I became a jerk. Angry and disheartened by what I saw in lackluster rehearsals, I careened into a horrible place called *bitter*.

"God, I hate Shaw," the director announced, laughing, at the first rehearsal of George Bernard Shaw's *Major Barbara*.

I was playing Barbara and, upon hearing this, wanted to kill myself. In the rehearsal hall, other actors chuckled. It was difficult for me to find anything funny in those days. This same director insisted the show be blocked in compliance with stage directions written over eighty years ago and for a proscenium arch stage. We would be performing on a three-quarter thrust stage.

Was he a complete moron? Quite possibly. I had become a snob about craft, and I was surely intolerable to be around.

"You're joking, right?" I spat.

The room became quiet and uneasy. I studied the faces of my cast mates, fairly seething as I burned into them. I was laying the trap for my own demise, having successfully achieved the status of pariah in the company.

The artistic director of the theatre took me aside with a warning. "*They* think *you* think you're better than they are."

"*They* are right," I shrugged.

I was worse than impolitic; I was a jackass. Maybe it was the theatres I was working in, maybe it was my increasingly uppity attitude, maybe it was just time . . . time to walk away because the joy had evaporated, and I was completely acidic to those unfortunate enough to be in my vicinity.

"Mel, where I studied, we were taught to learn our lines, learn our blocking, and open the show, not sit around asking questions about the character." This lecture came from the mouth of a young actor.

"I hope you sued your school."

I wasn't up for Miss Congeniality. The sarcasm trickled from my mouth like blood after a good punch.

It was the beginning of an agonizing crisis. Who was I, if not an actor? What would I, could I, do if not acting? What was my worth? And how would I ever replace the jolt of aliveness that being on center stage provided?

I'd never dated a man who didn't know me as an actor first. I was certain it was my work onstage that made me interesting. Offstage, I was nothing.

For months, as I wrestled with these questions, I slept. I rose in the morning, drank coffee, wrote in my journal, and began counting the hours until I could go back to bed. *Depressed* with a capital *D*.

I'd abandoned an ambition fueled from childhood. This was as torturous as surgery without anesthetic. Every day, I saw the blade and felt the cold slices.

A friend suggested I call a man, a man very familiar with Hollywood's rollercoaster of exhilaration and heartbreak. His name is Dennis Palumbo, and he was kind enough to take a desperate call from a woman at the end of her rope.

Dennis Palumbo was an A-list screenwriter who had decided to walk away from the klieg lights of film premieres to experience a different kind of life. He became a successful psychotherapist working with artists, among others. I described my state to him. I told him acting was the only way I knew how to make a living. The only way I knew how to live. I told him of my terror when I viewed the chasm that was supposed to be the rest of my life and how I wanted to die as I teetered over that crevice.

Dennis Palumbo threw me a lifesaver.

"You're always going to be an actor. Don't think of this as leaving acting—think of this as *adding to* your life as an actor. Other doors will present themselves to you when you open up to making your life bigger, not smaller."

His words bathed me like balm on the hottest of burns. He managed to disable the guilt I was holding onto as I considered a new life. He woke me up, and I was able to breathe after suffocating in mourning.

I still had no idea what I was going to do, but the panic was at bay, and I had relief.

Standing in Starbucks, the fear of that depression returning is real and present. A hungry fox is biting at my heels and heart. Surprisingly, spring break hasn't turned into much of a break. I fill my days with yoga, movies, books, and then more yoga and . . . I am adrift without those kids.

I miss them. I miss the struggles and my dream of doing the *Dream* and finding reasons to giggle within the difficulty of our even communicating with each other. What does Shakespeare mean to them? What good does it do? Beats me, but I have to get back there and do it better. Maybe I can help these kids experience the tenderness of a love scene or the rebellion of a willful daughter—and get a laugh or two while they're at it.

I take a hearty gulp of espresso. It's time to go back to Room 15 and do more, not less. I will coach them one on one. Yeah, that's a plan.

I have to get back to where I belong, where I am necessary.

CHAPTER XI

A LONELY BUSINESS

... Now I want
Spirits to enforce, art to enchant,
And my ending is despair,
Unless I be reliev'd by prayer ...

The Tempest Epilogue

He's the first one in, the first one to throw down his backpack, and the first one to sit in his chair. Miles, the changed boy.

He folds his hands on top of the script in his lap. He joins us in deep breathing. He demonstrates Child's Pose for the group. He hums as we hum. He repeats *toy boat*. He tries to catch a bumblebee in his mouth.

I have to tear my eyes away from the miracle in the room to give the others attention.

On the board:

HELP ME, LYSANDER, HELP ME! DO THY BEST
TO PLUCK THIS CRAWLING SERPENT FROM MY BREAST!
AY ME, FOR PITY! WHAT A DREAM WAS HERE!
LYSANDER, LOOK HOW I DO QUAKE WITH FEAR.

"William Shakespeare wrote most of his plays in verse, using a rhyming structure called iambic pentameter."

This is a mouthful to expect them to understand, but undeterred, I raise the bar.

I draw a rudimentary cup and sword and explain that iambic verse means ten beats to a line, with a sweet cup of cocoa being a soft beat and the strike of a sword being a hard beat.

"Shakespeare was telling us how to act his plays by showing us with these stresses what the most important thoughts were in a line."

I illustrate the stresses using Hermia's speech, sketching a cup over odd syllables and a sword over even syllables.

I ask who would like to come up and give it a try. Jennifer, eager to be the first, jumps up. I hand her the marker. She stares at the speech, then at me, then at the speech . . . back and forth, back and forth.

"Jennifer, break the first line up into syllables. Shakespeare always starts with a cup and ends with a sword."

"What's a syllable?" she asks.

Didn't see that one coming. "Okay, a syllable is—"

Clap CLAP clap CLAP—

I snap around and catch Candace smacking her hands together.

"Candace—" and I stop myself mid-shush. Candace is beating out syllables to help Jennifer.

"Help ME, Ly-SAN-der, HELP me! DO thy BEST!" *Clap CLAP clap CLAP clap CLAP clap CLAP clap CLAP.*

Candace has abandoned her hatred for Jennifer. The sniping and shoving have been replaced with—literal—helping hands. Candace is rescuing her enemy.

"Excellent, Candace. That's how we hear syllables."

Jennifer gets it and works out where a cup of cocoa sits next to a striking sword, and now, they all want a crack at the exercise. More of the speech goes on the board, and one by one, they give it a go.

These kids are learning scansion, the stuff of Shakespearean scholars.

This is what I can do: scan iambic verse, make a character come to life, hold an audience.

This is what I can't do: decipher algebra, hit a baseball, build a birdhouse . . .

———————————

As I was exiting my acting career, my lack of real-world skills became apparent. This was especially terrifying when the rent needed to be paid. I didn't have a college degree. Computers and I agreed to interact on a word-processing basis only. I was too old to waitress.

As panic began to stymie my sleep, a director I had worked with asked if I would coach a Japanese actress he was working with. My job would be to help with her English and her acting. She was a star in Japan, but she had to play an expatriate Japanese woman with an American sensibility.

"Sure," I said, quickly calculating how many rent checks this job would cover.

For several weeks, the actress and I met in her hotel room. She loved trashy Hollywood stories, so I had her read movie-star gossip rags and tell me what she'd learned. As she struggled to tell me the latest with Michael Jackson, her English improved.

I was with her every day on the film set and discovered I liked being on the other side of the camera. I didn't miss acting at all. Mixing with the crew was cool. Getting to know the grips, the camera department, the script supervisor, and the gaffer. It was a new kind of family, this crew.

Acting is a lonely business. On film sets, the crew prepares for hours while actors wait. The actors are alone and often scared because they want to be good, and they worry and stew about how to be good. After hours of trailer-sitting, they're called to the set, where they walk into blazing light and maybe the company of one or two other actors. Behind the lights is a crew hoping that the actors will hit their marks, get the shot, cry on cue, and do the job—and fast, because mess-ups cost time and time is expensive. Everyone wants to go home with something good in the can.

Acting is a solitary business riddled with anxiety.

Until I worked on the crew side, I didn't realize that. I was relieved of the pressure of working up my emotions to act. The price was relinquishing the thrill of applause, but for the first time, I could make that sacrifice because I'd found contentment helping someone else. If I used everything I knew about the craft to serve others, I could experience a different satisfaction.

I started a career as a dialogue coach on television and film sets while also coaching actors privately for auditions or upcoming jobs. I expanded my work to include public speaking for non-pros. It kept me in the loop with the stuff I loved about acting: the detective work that goes into creating a character, the curiosity about what people really do when crisis hits, the math of what makes funny . . . funny.

Dennis Palumbo was right. Once I opened myself to possibilities, they happened.

Back in the forest, I have ten actors and no Hermia since Regina quit. This is a puzzle I have struggled with over spring break. What to do, who to choose, and how to triple-cast some actors?

"Stella, I have good news and bad news. Which would you like first?" I hold her face in my hands.

"Bad!" she grins.

"You won't be playing Demetrius."

She screams, delighted. Again, didn't see that coming.

"What's the good news?" she shouts.

"If you promise never, *ever* to whine again, you can play Hermia."

Squeals and screeches bounce off the walls of Room 15. To describe Stella as excited would be an understatement.

The result of this casting coup: Stella never, ever whined in Shakespeare Club again. She didn't become an angel but, God bless her, she never complained after learning Hermia was hers.

HERMIA
Be it so, Lysander. Find you out a bed;
For I upon this bank will rest my head.

Stella attacks the verse like a pro. She owns the part from the moment she opens her mouth. She's brave, uses her big voice, and speaks to Lysander as if he is real, she is real, and the forest and grass are all real. An actor finding a home.

Miles, taken by Stella's powerful make-believe, allows himself to be swept along. When she tells him to lie down and sleep, he does. He lies on the floor with his hands crossed over his chest as if dead, but he does as he is told.

"Stella, why do you think Hermia tells Lysander to sleep apart from her?" I ask.

Stella giggles and looks at the corpse-like Miles. "Well . . . because they're just boyfriend and girlfriend, maybe?"

"That's right. Hermia knows they have to sleep separately until they're married. Here's a new plan: I'm going to be here on Tuesdays and Wednesdays after class to work with each of you alone on your scripts. Who wants to meet with me on Tuesday?"

They look at each other. *Don't everybody jump up at once.*

"Miles, how about you and I meet in the library at two-thirty on Tuesday? Ask your mom, and I'll be there. Bring your script."

Miles chews on the sleeve of his sweatshirt and gives a small nod.

"Anyone else?"

Marin's arm is up. "All right, Marin, you come too, and we'll work."

On Monday, I track Miles down to remind him about our date.

On Tuesday morning, I do the same.

"After school, Miles, in the library, okay?"

He nods.

On Tuesday afternoon, I sit alone in the library for an hour with two no-shows. I silently curse. *Where is the gratitude?*

I'm dragging my ego back to the car when I hear, "Ms. Ryane! Hey, Ms. Ryane!"

A solitary figure is standing in the courtyard, waving. I strain against the sunlight. *Who's that?*

"Hi!" he shouts, louder.

"Hi, Daniel." I stare. Is he mocking me? "How are you?"

"Good!" he shouts back. "Bye!" he cries over his shoulder as he takes off.

No hard feelings. I know it shouldn't matter, but cripes, he remembered me.

"Oh, Ms. Ryane, I'm so sorry," Marin says and blinks, very serious. "I forgot Tuesday is violin day." Both Marin and Grace are learning the violin in another after-school program.

"You're forgiven. We'll find another day to work."

Miles is not in the violin program. Miles is in the Miles program.

"Miles, what happened? I waited for you in the library for an hour on Tuesday."

"I forgot."

Miles is not forgiven.

CHILDREN'S WRITES

Dear Dairy,
I think that I had a beautiful character. Her name is Hermia. I reaaaaaallllllyyyyy like Shakespeare.
I always wanted to be a ater and now I am one.

LESSON PLAN

Raise the bar, ask more of them, and expect more. They want power; give it to them. Don't treat them like kids who can't. Treat them like kids who can.

THE VIOLIN PROGRAM

Before I became associated with the school, a first-grade teacher, Orlantha Ambrose, started an after-school program called "Strings by the Sea." She was also a concert-level violinist, and she wanted to teach children to play violin.

The program was a success, but Orlantha wanted to shake her life up and decided to return to the country of her parents' birth, Sri Lanka, to start a "Strings by the Sea" program with children there. In December of 2004, her parents went to visit her and hear her young students in concert. Orlantha's father, Dr. Anton Ambrose, then decided to take his wife, Beulah, and daughter to the seaside for a holiday.

One morning, while discussing breakfast with Beulah, Dr. Ambrose heard Orlantha in the next room.

"Mom! Dad! Water!"

The threesome ran from the tsunami. They made it out of their rooms, out of the lobby, and out of the hotel. Across the street, Dr. Ambrose found a truck to get them to safety. He glanced back and saw Beulah tying her shoe.

That was the last time he saw his wife alive.

He lost his wife and daughter that day. Dr. Ambrose survived by clinging for hours to a tree.

I wouldn't know what to do with so much sorrow, but I will tell you what Dr. Anton Ambrose did: he transformed the school's worn auditorium into the Orlantha Ambrose Center for the Performing Arts. He had it repainted and installed new floors and seats. He put in a lighting board and a sound system.

With his daughter's legacy, he gave children magic.

"I'm bored."

Even as Miles tries to step up to the plate in our rehearsals, there are days when he is plain bored while waiting for his time to speak. Stella toys with her fairy wreath. She isn't following along in her script . . . she's bored. All of them, in one way or another, love to let me know when they're *bored*.

Jordan tips her chair back and pretends to fall asleep. Marin, on top of a table, stares at the ceiling and whispers to Jennifer, who's lying next to her. They dangle their legs and kick the air like two girls stargazing on a camping trip.

Bored children.

A few years ago, I coached a child actor whose mother confessed she was worried about her daughter. She was concerned that her child might be ill because a terrific lethargy had set in. The girl would nod off in the car or at the dinner table. Her grades were dropping, and it perplexed the mom.

When I asked about the girl's schedule, I was told she was taking piano lessons, French immersion, tennis camp, dance class, and acting class. All of this in addition to homework, and she was also going on Hollywood auditions several times a week.

She was in fourth grade.

"She needs a nap," I said.

Actually, she needed more than that. She needed time to sit around and be bored. She needed time to lie on her bed and let her mind wander. She needed long summer days. Kids, inundated with information coming to them at warp speed, don't know how to slow down.

A study by the Proceedings of the National Academy of Sciences makes the case that educational toy buying is not the answer to building a fulfilling future for children. Flashcards and science kits won't necessarily create brainiacs. Maybe lying on the grass and counting clouds or doing nothing but getting bored may not be such a bad thing.

"Ms. Ryane, I'm bored!"

"Don't panic. Sometimes that's when really good ideas pop up."

"What ideas?"

"Maybe an idea on how to play your part."

Twiddling fingers, restless feet, twitching bodies . . .

"I'm bored."

"It'll pass."

CHAPTER XII

WHAT SHAKESPEARE MEANT BY *HAMLET*

To be, or not to be, that is the question . . . .
Hamlet Act III, Scene I

Her mom's sick."

"Her mom says she can't do Shakespeare Club anymore."

"She doesn't want to play Hermia."

Bingo. That's likely the truth, but so far, I'm running on rumors. I find Regina in the schoolyard, smashing a tetherball.

"Hey, Regina, got a sec?"

She holds the ball and eyes me skeptically.

"It's okay, you're not in trouble. I'm not mad or anything." She lets the ball drop.

I kneel beside her and wonder how it got to this point. Of all the kids in the club, Regina was the one I thought really wanted to act.

"So I'm hearing lots of scuttlebutt about why you quit, but I'm hoping you can tell me yourself."

"What's that mean, *scuttlestuff*?"

"That's another way of saying gossip."

"Well, I just want to go home and be with my mom and do my homework." Regina scans the horizon.

"There's nothing wrong with that."

"That's what I want to do." She peers at the dusty ground.

"I was worried you quit because you didn't want to play Hermia."

We both study the dust.

"Yeah, well . . ."

"Because, you know . . . if you wanted to be a fairy, that would be okay. We already have another Hermia."

"I just want to be with my mom and do homework after school."

"If you change your mind, let me know. Thursday, we're meeting in the auditorium to watch the movie, *Hamlet*. You're welcome to join us. Check with your mom, okay?"

"Okay . . . bye!" She scampers off to join her buddies.

I scuff the dirt with the toe of my shoe. Across the schoolyard, children in vibrant blues, yellows, reds, and pinks bob up and down, run and swing and slide. I feel as if I'm in the eye of a tornado. Calm and silent, but disturbed.

I lost another one. She swirled away from me.

———

At home in our kitchen, William helps me spoon freshly made popcorn into paper bags. It turns out that popcorn is nearly impossible to ladle. It flies around the room and scatters on the floor. Our dog heroically charges in to scoop up errant pieces. The entire enterprise is a mess, but I'm determined to make Movie Day a success. I line the bags up in a cardboard box along with juice cartons. All very orderly.

In the auditorium, the kids arrive and run up and down the aisles, clamber over seats, crawl on the stage, duck under the worn red stage curtain, and dash in and out of the bathrooms.

"Popcorn!" Marin screams. "She brought us popcorn!"

"Sit down!"

They ignore me.

"Popcorn and drinks!" Marin shouts.

"There will be no movie, no popcorn, and no drinks until you're all seated and ready to watch."

They take their seats. They want the popcorn.

I hand out the bags and juice and remind them of the story. "Hamlet is a prince who learns from his dead ghost dad that his father was murdered by his uncle."

"A real ghost?" Jordan asks, incredulous.

"Absolutely. Hamlet starts to act crazy. He tells his girlfriend, Ophelia, that she should be a nun. He convinces actors to act out a story of the murder to test his uncle's reaction. There's a big swordfight, his mom is poisoned, Ophelia's brother is stabbed, and Hamlet dies after killing the uncle. The end."

"Ms. Ryane, did this really happen?"

"I'm happy to see you here, Regina. And no, this is a made-up story."

"How do you know so much about Hamlet?" Regina asks.

"Once upon a time, I played Ophelia, so I got to know it pretty well then."

"Do you mean when *you* were a kid, *you* were in Shakespeare Club?" Candace asks.

Hmmm. I wonder if I *were* a kid in Shakespeare Club, which one of them I would be. An outsider like Dana? Check. As shy as Grace? Check. Spitting with anger like Candace? Check. As challenging as Miles? I smile. I of all people should understand his behavior, after spending all those days in that cloak-room.

"When I was a kid, we didn't have Shakespeare Club. I only wanted to read books and go to my dance class, but Mom also made me play softball."

"She *made* you?" Anna asks.

The sun blazed down, making my hair hot to the touch. I looked at my stupid, stupid shoes. They weren't even sneakers. They were canvas beach shoes, too small for my growing feet. Mom had cut holes in them to add space for my toes. Sandal wannabes.

At least in the outfield I was far away from the other players . . . and my mom in the stands, watching me hard. The summer air rang with shouts from fans.

"Pitcha's gotta rubber arm!"

"Batta, batta, batta swing!"

"Hey, ho, time to go!"

The giant mitt on my hand looked like a science experiment gone awry. I banged the hard leather against my bony leg and placed my heels together with toes pointed outward to make ballet first position. I lifted my right foot and tried to bend it into a pointed arch, but the stiff rubber sole of the stupid, stupid shoe wouldn't yield. I set my foot on the grass and bent into first-position plié, then moved into second-position plié. Right arm extended, left arm in a gentle curve with the fat, tawny glove hanging off the end—

In the distance, the crowd's chants turned into one long scream of "Meeelllll . . . Mel . . . Mel . . . !"

I glanced up, and my glasses reflected glimmers of the summer sun and—*boink!*—the ball bounced off my shoulder. *Ow.* Dazed, I watched the ball roll away until I recovered and gave chase, trapping it with the clumsy glove.

"Throw it!"

"Throw, throw, throw!" my teammates screeched.

I pulled my arm back, ready to throw to the infield, when I saw her, face dropped into her hands and shame red as blood dripping through her clutched fingers. *She's trying to erase the image of me. She wants another girl to be her daughter.* She wouldn't look at me, and I knew we were in for a silent night.

My throw was feeble, and the ball dribbled to the vicinity of the shortstop.

At home, our shelves were filled with golden statues of Mom's amateur softball career. On each trophy, a tiny player in a cap posed with bat held high or arm pulled back, ready to send a pitch over the plate. I caressed the shiny outlines of these miniature athletes frozen in play.

On warm spring evenings, my dad would pack us in the car to get to "the game." Mom, dressed in her freshly washed green and white uniform, sat in the front seat massaging her glove, ready to jump from the car and get to her team.

When I think back on my mom as she pitched and hit, shouted and laughed, it's clear she was as alive as she could possibly be. This was her world. This was where she mattered. After a game, she instructed Dad to take us three kids home while she celebrated with "just a couple of beers" with her team. This was how Mom escaped her life as a wife and mother. She lived for the grimy dust of the diamond and the physical demands of swinging, sliding, and catching.

I didn't embrace this world.

"You're anti-social," she'd tell me. "You have no friends, you're always holing up with some book . . . it's not healthy. I'm signing you up for a team. It'll be fun; *I* love it . . . you'll see."

And I did see.

"Anyone who doesn't want to be in Shakespeare Club shouldn't be in it," I say softly. "No hard feelings. I don't want you to be like I was on the softball team."

I have my hand on the auditorium light switch. "Ready?"

"Yes!" they cry. I flick the lights off and join them in the dark.

On screen, Mel Gibson wanders the rooms of a grey, cold Danish castle in director Franco Zeffirelli's film version of *Hamlet*. Miles, sitting beside me, doesn't fidget and barely remembers to eat his popcorn. He's rapt, watching the ghost scene.

"Ms. Ryane," he whispers. I lean in close.

"If we ever do *Hamlet*, I want to play Hamlet. I get this. I get the ghost is his dad, and Hamlet's really, really mad at his uncle. He wants to kill him, he's so mad, right?" With big brown eyes, he looks up at me for confirmation.

"Yes, Miles, he is that mad."

At the back of the auditorium, girls are running in and out of the bathroom. I march back and swing open the door. Stella, Regina, and Carla giggle in a huddle.

"What's going on, girls?"

They look at each other, but no one answers.

"You said you wanted to see this movie, now go sit and watch it." I sport a grim look to show that I mean it. "Otherwise, off you go to the playground."

Zeffirelli has decided that Hamlet has an Oedipal relationship with his mother. In the scene where Hamlet berates Gertrude for her marriage to Claudius, his behavior is, well, illustrative of that.

"We have to fast-forward," I explain, "or we won't be able to see the whole movie. This is where Hamlet is mad at his mom for marrying his uncle."

I use the remote to buzz through the Hamlet/Gertrude scene. Images of Hamlet wrestling with his mother speed across the screen. He rips her dress as they grapple.

"Ms. Ryane," Marin demands, "why is Hamlet kissing his mom on the mouth?"

I could simply wring Mr. Zeffirelli's neck.

"Um . . . well . . . he's just acting like a lunatic. Remember I told you how he wants everyone to think he's nuts?"

"But why is her dress all ripped and he kissed her on the *mouth*?"

"Marin, you can see they live in a drafty, cold castle . . ." I strain for an explanation. "People were more, um, affectionate with their parents back in those days."

Marin's eyes burn into me.

"Oh, look, look, Marin! You don't want to miss this part. Gertrude, the queen, is about to drink the poison and die . . . this is really exciting!"

I don't look at Marin, willing her to return to the movie, but she's locked on me like a cobra hunting a mouse.

"On the *mouth*, Ms. Ryane?" Her eyebrows are raised as if *she's* the teacher.

I can't respond because I'm struck in the head by pieces of popcorn zipping through the air. As the film loses its pizzazz, a food fight unfolds.

"All right, knock it off! If this is what you want to do with your popcorn, I won't even bother to make it when we see another movie."

"What other movie?" Stella shouts.

"*Nanny McPhee!*" Jordan yells.

"*Spider-Man!*" Miles shouts.

I'm bitter and jumpy, not unlike poor Gertrude. She's overwhelmed by Hamlet in the same way I am by these kids. There's going to be popcorn crud underfoot, and I'll be in trouble for corrupting children with a sicko scene with Hamlet and his mother.

"Well, look at that, four o'clock, time for you to go." They race out, banging each other in the doorway like hockey players. I eject the DVD and replace it in its case.

"Ms. Ryane?" I turn around.

Regina has her pink backpack slung over one shoulder.

"Hey, what's up?"

"Can I come back to Shakespeare Club?"

"Of course you can."

"But I don't want to be Hermia."

"No problem. You don't have to be Hermia, but I expect you to be a really good fairy and to read the chorus parts with everyone else. Can you manage that?"

She nods with a smile.

"See you next Thursday then."

"Okay." She takes off.

Why does she want to come back? Why do any of them?

Juice boxes and wayward bits of popcorn litter the floor, but a miniature janitorial staff is hard at work. Marin and Grace have stayed behind to sweep the aisles with long brooms. They lift the seats, scoop up garbage, and dump it into trashcans. I didn't ask them to do this. I'm stunned by the initiative of these children.

When they're done, they grab their belongings and start to leave.

"Girls, thank you. I really appreciate your doing that."

"Okay," Marin says. "Bye!"

"See ya, Ms. Ryane!" Grace cries. And off they charge.

Walking to my car, I run into Miles.

"Is your mom coming to pick you up?"

He nods.

"So, Hamlet. What a guy, huh?"

"Yeah."

"Miles, I'll certainly think about *Hamlet* for next year, but if you want to be considered for that part, you need to put more effort into Lysander."

"Yeah."

"Do you want to show up for a private work session in the library with me?"

"Yeah."

"Next Tuesday after school, okay?"

"Yeah."

Miles is a man of few words.

"There's my mom," he says, ambling to the car.

He climbs into the front seat. His mom chats away as she checks her mirrors. Miles has his forehead pressed against the window, and he studies the gravel as they pull away.

Good night, sweet prince.

Did I just say *next year*?

CHILDREN'S WRITES

— *I thot hamlet was a graet movie because of the poson.*

— *I think Hamlet was boring. It had no action, no suspens, no love, and no*

— *To me think that was very sad, because knowing that your uncle killed you own dad and know you uncle married your mother.*

— *I think Hamlet was boring and nacity. I couldn't understand the words.*

— *It was sad because he's dad died. He find out about he's new dad kill he's dad.*

— *The movie was cool. More better then Barny. Movie was good. Hamlet is brave.*

LESSON PLAN

They are not you.

Again, Miles is a no-show on Tuesday.

According to the gossipmongers, "He said he didn't want to come. He just wanted to fool around."

According to Miles, "I forgot."

Play baseball. Play Lysander. Play soccer. Play Hamlet.

I'm across a library table from Grace. We have our scripts open to Puck.

"Grace, you have my favorite line in the play. In fact, I think your line is the theme of the play. Puck says, 'Lord, what fools these mortals be.'"

Grace grins.

"Puck is a fairy. A fairy can do anything, like fly around the world or be invisible and spy on people. A fairy can do magic tricks."

Grace's smile grows.

"Imagine if we could do all those things. I guess, for a fairy, real people seem kind of silly."

Grace opens and closes her mouth as if she wants to tell me something.

"What is it?"

"I have a Globe Theatre!"

"What do you mean?"

"I found it in a store, and my mom let me buy it. I built it."

"And where is it?"

"By my bed."

"So, you have a model of Shakespeare's Globe Theatre?"

Grace bobs her head up and down, beaming.

"That's really cool."

Grace and I work on Puck. I help her with words she doesn't understand. I tell her Puck wants to please Oberon, her master, and I encourage her to use her big voice. But Grace is a shy eight-year-old. She doesn't misbehave in our club meetings. She's quieter than the others. She doesn't have the force of Marin or Dana or Stella. It doesn't seem important to Grace to be the most popular or the funniest.

She will, however, be the first actor to learn her lines.

Grace runs across the schoolyard when she sees me to recite her Puck lines. She works hard on her script, and though she will never have the showmanship of the others, she's able to connect to her little Globe Theatre as if she can shrink herself and crawl into a wondrous world of long ago.

By spring, she tells me, "Me and Marin are going to do Shakespeare Club next year."

She keeps repeating it, as if I might forget. As if to remind me she'd made a commitment, and so must I.

Grace has gently nagged me not to give up.

CHAPTER XIII

THE ACTOR'S BURDEN

I prithee peace, my soul is full of sorrow.
Richard III Act II, Scene I

NARRATOR
Peter Quince and his actors gather to rehearse their play. Puck will use his magic on Nick Bottom.

Candace, in the middle of Room 15, is wearing the furry donkey mask. She slouches with one hand on her right hip and fixes me with dark eyes through holes in the mask. Candace is an unhappy Bottom. She looks at the script and shakes her head. I search my text for the problem.

BOTTOM
Why do they run away? This is to make an ass of me: to fright me.

"I can't say that." Her voice is cold.

"What?"

"You know . . . and I'm not saying it now either!" She's a cauldron of furry fury.

"Candace, it means *donkey*. It's in the Bible. It's not a curse word in this play."

"No, no, no!"

"Fine, let's skip that part for now and move onto 'Hee haw, hee haw.' Pick it up where you say, 'I will walk up and down and will sing that they shall hear I am not afraid.'"

She refuses to speak, switching her rage to her other hip. Her shiny blue BABY GIRL jacket is zipped up to her neck, her hair pulled into a ponytail with loose tendrils around her face. Like a bad storm, her eyes darken through the donkey face.

"Go on." My voice is soft.

"Hee haw, hee haw . . ." she mumbles. She refuses to participate in our rehearsal in any joyful fashion. The actress she was a few weeks ago has all but disappeared.

I don't know why Candace is angry today. During spring break, the twins were sent to their grandmother's house up the coast in Oxnard. Upon returning, Jordan reported they would be moving to a new place in a few weeks. The clue to Candace's behavior could be hidden in these plans. I don't think her anger is at me, or the play, or the group. She's just lost her footing. Her mistrust seems enormous.

As Titania, Anna is lying at Candace's feet. Anna ignores the donkey's sullen mood, behaving as if everything is fine. She adjusts her pink boa and delivers her line.

TITANIA
What angel wakes me from my flow'ry bed?
I pray thee, gentle mortal, sing again.

Anna's effort is a reminder that some days, repairs aren't possible. Some days, we carry on under painful burdens, some days less so. Candace slumps to her seat at the end of the scene. She covers her face with her script and swivels her back to me. She's as closed as a clam. I want to make things better, to give her a silver lining and make every happy cliché work for Candace, but that's not going to happen. Not today.

A fifth-grade teacher advised me: "Mel, I've had to accept that each of these kids is wrestling with issues."

At first, I wasn't sure what she meant. Then I considered Candace's pain next to Miles's antics, Stella's relentless whining, and Regina's fear of failure, and her words made sense.

Across the room, Dana's hunger for fame and Carla's reluctance to read aloud compete with Marin's need to knock others out of her way.

Just like the characters in Shakespeare's plays, these kids are indeed wrestling with issues. They long for power, revenge, and love. On school grounds across the nation, battles erupt every day over the need for power, revenge, and love.

And sadly, often for food.

The task of feeding these kids in a responsible manner during our meetings has eluded me. I lay out food and assume they can apportion it in reasonable fashion. It's taken me longer than it should have to see that I need to hand out equal allotments.

With my back turned, they attack the snacks like starved barbarians. Hands, feet, and elbows fly at all angles as food is grabbed, stuffed, and devoured in record time. An entire pizza can disappear in a matter of seconds. The children of Shakespeare Club make the cast of *Oliver Twist* look like highbrow swells.

Candace is closed up and cut off. She rips off the donkey mask and tosses it aside. Curled up in her chair, she looks trapped. And I don't know how to rescue her.

My desire to become an actor wasn't fed so much by talent as it was by desperation. It was a masterstroke of rebellion as well as a blueprint for escape.

I became a nurse *and* a doctor without ever opening a medical text. Paid to act those roles, I flaunted it in the face of those who had mocked me by asking, "Who do you think you are?" and "What made you think you could leave this house and do *that*?"

At eighteen, I ran away to join a circus called the theatre. I begged actors and teachers to help me. In rehearsal halls, I hung around long after my scenes were done to watch the pros. I copied the vocal cadences of sophisticates and trilled my voice at the end of a joke, or dropped it low with a tidbit of gossip. I dumped my youth into the laps of the seasoned, becoming a ready audience for their tutelage. I hitched my cart to the carnival barkers of Shakespeare, Shaw, and Coward.

I wore what the pros wore, drank what they drank, and ate food unheard of in the suburbs of my upbringing. I ordered sweetbreads and hearts of palm and chased them with champagne cocktails. I quaffed Gin Fizzes and Pimm's No. 1 Cups. I grooved to jazz and boogied in Montreal's gay discos. I lit my cigarettes the cool way, striking a match on the sole of my boot. I was somebody, alright, adopted into a family that trained me like a new puppy.

When my parents showed up backstage, I treated them like Ma and Pa Kettle. I leaned against the dressing room door to make sure they couldn't get inside. I didn't want them to contaminate my world. Disdain dripped from my pores when I muttered, "Hey, nice to see you . . . I'll catch you in the morning for breakfast . . . have to go . . . see ya later."

And I disappeared, taking off to the nearest bar to join my idols gathered after the show. Legendary actors brimming with stories of lives spent on the

boards. These were my heroes, and they let me be with them. Actors who traveled town to town in their caravans of verse and Scotch.

I rarely showed up to those promised breakfasts with my parents. Unaware,
I couldn't see I was exacting punishment for years of "there she goes, the little
actress" and "so misunderstood, poor Mel, the crybaby."

Whatever I was doing to them felt really good. Revenge can be like that.

My parents returned the snub by never, ever mentioning my work. After
seeing me perform, they'd sing the praises of every other actor onstage except
me. Years later, after I'd left the profession, my father made a suggestion.

"Why don't you go back to acting?" As he tilted his head to watch the clouds
pass, he had an afterthought. "You were so good at it."

That's news to me, Dad. Did you always think this? I'll never know . . . and
I'm still too afraid to ask.

"Hey, Ms. Ryane!" I tear my eyes away from the morose Candace and spot her
sister's eager face.

"Yes, Jordan?"

"Who's Demetrius?"

This is a problem I haven't yet solved. Demetrius was Daniel, then Stella.
But Stella has taken on Hermia, and now we're short a Demetrius. *Think fast.
Don't look weak.* I skim through the roles in my head and hope I can assign the
part without creating a catastrophe. It's tricky. We can't have actors talking to
themselves in the same scene.

Every pair of eyes is on me, waiting for an answer.

"Jordan, I think it would work if you played Demetrius."

She leaps and cheers. The goal is no longer *what* part one is playing, but *how
many* parts. Jordan now has two.

Stella trots to center stage with Jordan, who is ready to play Demetrius. Stella
relishes the words and belts them out in amusing gung-ho spirit.

HERMIA
What's this to my Lysander? Where is he?
Ah, good Demetrius, wilt thou give him me?

DEMETRIUS
I had rather give his carcass to my hounds.

HERMIA
Out, dog! Out cur! Thou driv'st me past the bounds
Of maiden's patience.

I want these kids to experience how personal traumas can serve their work. Oh, Candace. Isolated across the room, she ignores us and scuffs the toe of her shoe into the floor again and again and again.

Dana hikes her jeans over her protruding tummy and strolls to the center of the room. She shoots an evil eye to Grace with a *pssst!* Grace scurries into place, offering an apologetic look to me for her late entrance. I nod and smile.

OBERON
This falls out better than I could devise.
But hast thou yet latched the Athenian's eyes
With the love juice, as I did bid thee do?

Dana towers over Grace, demanding an answer. Grace faces front and recites her line.

PUCK
This is the woman, but not this the man.

I give Grace a thumbs-up, and Dana, noticing my encouragement, attacks Puck with unprecedented vehemence.

OBERON
What hast thou done?

I know how Dana feels about "the little kids" and give her a thumbs-up as well. Our stage area has filled up as Demetrius and Lysander traipse after Helena to proclaim their love. Jennifer, a willow of a girl who doesn't believe herself beautiful, is perfect for Helena, who thinks herself ugly.

"Jennifer, when you act, use your outside voice. The audience doesn't know this story, and you'll help them by speaking up."

"Okay," she whispers. On her next attempt, she struggles and can't quite get there. Her approach is delicate, soft, and self-conscious.

HELENA
O spite! O hell! I see you all are bent
To set against me for your merriment.

Jordan kneels in front of Jennifer and pleads for love. Miles copies Jordan and also begs for Jennifer's affection, but he's holding his script in front of his face. It's ridiculous, but I'm grateful that he's even reading his lines out loud.

DEMETRIUS
I say I love thee more than he can do.

LYSANDER
If thou say so, withdraw and prove it too.

And here it is. The moment Miles has been waiting for. He turns to me, eyebrows raised. A promise is a promise is a promise. . . .

Out of the Shakespeare Club box, I lift the shiny plastic swords with gold plastic handles, as if removing them from a glass case in the British Museum. Miles trembles, hands held upward and, in the tradition of young King Arthur, I lay the sword onto his damp palms with ceremony.

"We know what this means, right, Miles?"

His face is grave, and he nods.

"Use it wisely, as Lysander would."

He caresses the cheap costume shop prop.

Stella makes a display of being terribly upset as she confronts Lysander. She hunches her shoulders when demanding an explanation.

HERMIA
Why are you grown so rude! What change is this,
Sweet love?

Because they're cousins and live in close proximity, Stella, Jennifer, and Miles bug each other on a regular basis. Now the behavior has a place on Shakespeare's stage.

Miles has stuck his weapon in a belt loop of his jeans. Emboldened, he shouts:

LYSANDER
Ay, by my life!
'Tis no jest that I do hate thee, and love Helena.

Invigorated by Miles, Jennifer finds some volume and joins in to attack Hermia.

HELENA
Fie, fie! You counterfeit, you puppet, you!

Stella sucks up the humiliation and unloads on a confused Helena.

HERMIA
Puppet! Ay, that way goes the game.
And you are grown so high in his esteem,

Because I am so dwarfish and so low?
How low am I, thou painted maypole? Speak!

And, in what would become Miles's favorite moment of the play, he attacks Hermia.

LYSANDER
Get you gone, you dwarf, you bead, you acorn!

Then he falls to the floor, roaring with laughter. Imagine being encouraged to insult your cousin. Life for Miles is just getting better and better.

These children are giving voice to their own complicated stories. Instructed by their parents to play nice, they fight for distance and privacy at school and home. Some days, their irritations are open sores, red and raw.

At the end of the school year, Jennifer confesses to me that she won't be in Shakespeare Club again because her family is moving "to a big farm in Mexico, where my dad says I can have a pony and a goat and a dog and my own room." Jennifer will get space.

When I ask Miles if he'll miss his cousin, he answers, "Now I get her room."

We finish our first satisfactory rehearsal, but something had occurred that I neither saw nor heard. I would learn about it much later. A fissure had opened, and it would end in sadness.

I'm relieved and thrilled we've made our way through so many pages of the script. They're really starting to comprehend the text. This could work.

As I lock up Room 15, I glimpse Dana plodding away, shoulders sagging.

"Hey, Dana!"

She turns to me with a silent, bitter glare.

Taken aback, I stammer, "Good work today . . . it's really coming along. . . ."

Dana shrugs and marches off.

I replay the rehearsal in my mind. There's an annoying wisp of something . . . what is it? What happened, and did I really want to know?

"Hey, Ms. Ryane!"

I'm unlocking my car as I hear the familiar voice.

"Hey, Daniel." I wave. "How's it going?"

"Good!" he yells. "See ya!"

I don't know anything. They're all a mystery to me.

CHILDREN'S WRITES

Dear Dairy,

   My faviote characters were Lysander and Demetrus. I was Lysander in the play. My enimne was Demetrus. They are my favriote carecters because they are brave and they had swords. And those are my favriote carectors.

LESSON PLAN

Teachers don't actually have eyes in the backs of their heads. Things will be missed. It's unavoidable.

On Tuesday, Jordan shows up for a private session in the library. We don't talk about Candace. I'm hoping Jordan's enthusiasm will inspire her sister.

These girls are a tag-team of moods. When one is up, the other is down and vice versa. It's slippery and impossible to guess where they'll be on any given day.

"Jordan, here's a fun part about acting: you get to do and say things onstage that you can't always get away with in real life."

She studies the script and her role as Peter Quince.

"You see how Peter Quince gets to be mad at Nick Bottom and put him in his place? In real life, we're not allowed to stamp our feet and throw temper tantrums, but that's exactly what you can do when you're acting. I say go for it."

She grins and tries out a speech.

QUINCE
   No, no; you must play Pyramus; and Flute, you Thisby.

A bit underplayed, but we're only beginning. I read Bottom and give her cues as she works up the courage to state her case.

"Jordan, stand up. Try this on your feet. I want you to really give me *what for* with these lines. You can be as nasty as you want."

This is a serious challenge for a young girl acting opposite an adult. It's one thing to behave aggressively with her sister, but across from me, it's tricky business. Jordan adjusts her jeans, her sweatshirt, and her posture. It can be difficult to get comfortable on the high board before a dive.

QUINCE
Answer as I call you. Nick Bottom, the weaver.

BOTTOM
Ready. Name what part I am for, and proceed.

QUINCE
You, Nick Bottom, are set down for Pyramus.

"Jordan, think about when you're angry. Like when no one will listen to you, or when you're blamed for something you didn't do."

At the library table, she lays her head on folded hands. Have I gone too far? What is she digging up?

In a flash, she stands up, gives me a firm look, stomps her foot, and yells, "You will play no part but Pyramus!"

Her face registers shock. We burst out laughing.

"And that, my friend, is what they call acting! Fun, huh?"

We pack up and leave the library. Candace, slumped at a picnic table, waits for her sister.

"Hey, Candace, do you want to do some work with me?"

"Nope." She slides away, slinging her backpack over her shoulder.

There was always a morning after, and another show, followed by another bar scene, and so on and so on. The dawn brought an upset stomach and a nagging headache. These maladies were easily remedied with Maalox and aspirin, two requisite items next to the powder and grease paint in an actor's kit bag.

But nothing could fill the ghostly silence of a stark hotel room. Paper-thin walls resounded with the sexy wails of someone else's one-night stand and kept me in bed with a pillow over my head. I found no relief from the emptiness of an actor's life on the road. As sweet as the party started, in the end, I couldn't stand an existence sustained only by the love of an audience of strangers.

"Candace . . . wait!" I hurry to catch up to her. Her face is near expressionless.

I put my hand on her shoulder, "No more pouting . . . deal?"

Candace tilts her head, considers, and in a flat voice answers, "Deal." She lopes off.

That went well. I think.

Jordan runs after Candace and glances back with a wave and a shrug. I'm a little comforted. The twins are twins. For now, that may be the solace that gets them up each day to try again.

———

Revenge is sweet. Don't get angry, get even. These aphorisms are rolling around in my head on the drive home.

"Do you ever want revenge?" I ask William as I open our front door.

"All the time."

"Me too." I drop my books and open a bottle of wine.

"Went that well?"

"Actually, it did go pretty well, but revenge is in the air, and I don't think I can stop it. Did you ever get revenge?"

"Never. But I like thinking about it." He pours.

"Me too," I sigh and take a sip.

At least we can talk about it. The kids in Shakespeare Club don't even know they want revenge. They don't even know they're angry.

The hidden bomb is the more dangerous one.

CHAPTER XIV

WAR DECLARED

When have I injur'd thee? When done thee wrong?
Or thee? or thee? or any of your faction?
A plague upon you all!

Richard III Act I, Scene III

Room 15 has been yanked from us, and we've been temporarily sent back to the library. Repairs of some sort have rendered us homeless, and my stomach is tight. I don't want to return to the library, where pillows flew last autumn. But here we are, gathered around tables to read the play.

"What?" Carla cries. "From the beginning *again*? We already did that!"

"Rehearsal means going back over parts we've done. It's common for actors to do this. This is how we become more familiar with the story."

"But we haven't even finished acting to the end," Stella moans.

"That's correct, but we can't block the play here in the library, so we're going to read it, no arguments. Even though we can't walk around in here, how about you stand when you speak? Let's make the goal of today's rehearsal to really talk to each other like real people in real life."

I've placed their scripts where I want them to sit because I'm hyper-aware of the continuing animosities between certain kids. Dana has ducked behind a bookshelf with Miles on the other side. She crams herself behind the half-wall and speaks past him, not to him. They look like characters in an espionage thriller sharing a veiled exchange. Dana appears to do this for my benefit, giving me a conspiratorial nod.

Is she trying to signal something? I'm going to ignore her for the moment.

However, the gauntlet has been thrown, and I make a private note. There will be no "really talking to each other like real people" because Dana and Miles refuse to even look at each other.

We meander our way through a dismal stumble-through. The mood has been set by Dana's stubbornness, and nearly everyone picks up on it. Marin mumbles her lines, Stella refuses to shut up while others are speaking, and Miles eyes the bottoms of the tables. He slides down his chair, eyes on me, and just as his butt is about to touch the floor, I shake my head. Like a spool of film in rewind, he scoots back up, smirking.

Candace has ignored our verbal deal of "no pouting" and maintains an indifference to both me and the play. Jordan whispers Demetrius' lines, rendering last week's breakthrough moot. Grace, Regina, and Carla giggle, tickle, and kick each other. Jennifer has subdued her voice again, and we're once more dependent on Anna's professional demeanor to hold on to a tattered plot.

The library is a boiler room of frustrated energy as adversaries claim their territory.

Handing out pencils and colored pens, I hope we can at least accomplish some journal writing. Next week, back in Room 15, we'll find our groove with a proper rehearsal.

As the meeting draws to a close, I collect scripts and pack the Shakespeare Club box. Because I'm busy, the kids take the opportunity to go berserk and crawl underneath desks and inside reading cubicles, where they scream, shriek, and do everything but write. Anna, alone, remains writing at her table. The rest have launched an all-out war.

Dana rises from behind a wall and hurls a paper ball at Miles. She's used paper ripped from her journal, and fury blazes through me like wildfire. I have shopped so carefully for these notebooks, and now they're making garbage out of them along with the pens and scripts and time and parties and movies and popcorn . . . . *Where the hell is the gratitude?*

"Stop! Stop it right now and get back to your seats!"

From each cubicle, like brats in foxholes, they peer back, grinning. I don't grin back. They're not adorable, and I'm completely fed up.

"Dana, drop the paper! Now!" I glare at her.

Dana makes a grave mistake.

"But Ms. Ryane, the little kids were throwing balls at me and I didn't do anything."

"Dana, I'm a lot of things, but I'm not an idiot and I'm certainly not blind."

"No, Ms. Ryane, I wasn't doing anything!"

"Dana, I saw you. I'm right here in front of you. I saw you throw the paper, so don't even *try* to claim otherwise."

Big tears fill her eyes, and I'm astonished as she sticks with her story.

"No, Ms. Ryane, the little kids were throwing paper, but I wasn't."

Rage courses through me. I take a breath and take aim directly into her watery orbs.

"Dana, you're lying to me. I saw you throw the paper, which means you ripped up your journal to do it. I saw you, so you cannot tell me you didn't do it. I'm not saying no one else did the same thing, but I'm *telling* you I *saw* you."

"But, Ms. Ryane, really, it wasn't me . . . ." She trails behind me as I turn away, motioning for everyone to get up, get their stuff, and get out.

I remember an earlier discussion about how Mr. Davis had kicked her out of choir because "he said I *did* and I *didn't*," and I recall how bad I felt for her that day. How she seemed so misunderstood. I believed her. I urged her to talk to Mr. Davis and iron things out. I bought her crap story complete with those ready-for-my-close-up droplets falling from her eyes.

Dana is duplicitous, and she may carry the DNA of Richard III, but today, she shares the stage with another formidable actor. I'm instantly plucked out of Oz and my romantic notions of a little project called the Shakespeare Club. My initiation is complete. As the scope of this young girl's deception dawns on me, I feel foolish and naive.

If teachers drink, I now know why. Kids aren't cute.

———————

In seventh grade, one of our subjects was Library, a period spent listening to our school librarian trill arias on the Dewey Decimal System. Mrs. Felton, a slight woman, fluttered her dry, bony hands as she sang the praises of Salinger and Steinbeck. I have no idea why, but occasionally, Mrs. Felton would get me out of math to work in the library. Which was fantastic, since I hated math. And science, and history, and gym, among other subjects.

Mrs. Felton set me up in a large closet with the task of copying illustrations of Laura Ingalls Wilder's homesteaders or Beatrix Potter's bunnies onto poster board using an overhead projector. This effort required absolutely no talent. I simply traced what the projector illuminated. After a picture was finished, Mrs. Felton would *oooh* and *aaah* before hanging it on the wall.

I was thrilled Mrs. Felton chose me to do this. It was as if the hand of God himself had rescued me from the studies I despised. Alone in that dark closet with only the light from the projector and its comforting whirr, I traced and painted.

Mrs. Felton gave me a gift for which I showed no gratitude. To seventh graders, Library was a free period, a party class, a chance to gossip, slouch, spew bad language, and create mayhem.

Cutouts of the Beatles and David Cassidy covered our notebooks. Girls decorated theirs with hearts and curlicues, boys with lightning bolts and 3-D block letters spelling out the names of various narcotics. We scrawled *peace* across every surface. Ask Mrs. Felton if we had an iota what *peace* meant as we posed with our fingers in the V symbol.

Testosterone and other renegade hormones pinged off bookshelves as if we were all caught inside a giant pinball machine. And she was trapped with us, poor, banged-up, pathetic Mrs. Felton and her whimsical fantasies of teaching eager children the merits of fine literature.

Is this what Mrs. Felton imagined when she graduated with degrees in education and library science?

"Quiet and order," she warbled in a voice straining to overcome our thunderous din.

One afternoon, Mrs. Felton was hit with one too many spitballs, and she combusted. With our rowdiness reaching a screeching pinnacle, Mrs. Felton crumpled into her chair with forehead cupped in her hands. She shrank, tinier and tinier, behind a desk that looked to engulf her. Tears flowed down her cheeks and rolled down her skinny, blue-veined arms. Her shoulders shook as we gradually fell into stunned silence. It was the only time the library was quiet. The only sound in the library was Mrs. Felton sobbing.

Thirty kids watched her with the paralysis usually reserved for a good movie. We didn't consider ourselves participants in this drama; we saw ourselves as kids and her as an adult. This was how the roles were to be played until the day Mrs. Felton changed the script and had a nervous breakdown.

Mrs. Felton never again stepped into that school. My days in a closet with an overhead projector ended, and I knew I was culpable in the death of her teaching career. I had run with the pack, and I had never said thank you. It was intoxicating to hang with the cool kids, and now I was one of the criminals.

No, kids aren't cute.

Before they leave the school library, I announce, "Whoever wants to do private work should be here on Tuesday or Wednesday after school."

"Me, me!" Stella cries.

"All right, Stella, I'll see you here Tuesday."

Marin signs up, along with Jennifer and Anna.

"Yeah, maybe I will," Miles says.

"Forget it, Miles. Either yes or no. I won't be stood up again."

"Yeah, okay." He leaves.

I have no idea what that means, and I don't care. I really don't care if I see any of them again.

They're meek as they depart. They gather backpacks and exit in silence.

"Bye, Ms. Ryane," Jennifer whispers.

"Uh-huh."

I collapse into a chair. I'm on the brink of a Mrs. Felton episode. How do real teachers do this every day? Our routine has become one good meeting followed by three terrible ones. I'm either in euphoria or despair. *Why am I so lousy at this?*

The group has divided into warring factions: Dana, Candace, and Jordan, the fifth graders. Jennifer and Marin, the fourth graders. Grace, Stella, Carla, and Regina, the third graders. Miles, the lone male, is a solitary soldier. Anna, snubbed by the others, hasn't aligned with anyone.

1. WE HELP EACH OTHER.
2. WE SHARE WITH EACH OTHER.
3. WE HONOR THE WORKS OF WILLIAM SHAKESPEARE.

They kneel in Child's Pose, breathe deep, and repeat vocal exercises, but I'm a complete nincompoop to imagine any of this resonates or means anything to them. Share with each other? These kids want to kill each other. And today, I wanted to kill all of them and then myself.

I shuffle out of the library, shifting the stupid damn-it-to-hell Shakespeare Club box from hip to hip. As I'm about to open the car trunk, I hear a voice.

"Ms. Ryane!"

Stella runs up, full of pep. I give her a nod. It's all I'm capable of. I wish I were driving away.

"Guess what? Listen! 'So will I grow, so live, so die!'" she shouts.

I nod and slam the trunk.

"See I learned it . . . I learned it by heart!" She sparkles.

I examine the car keys in my hands. "Stella, that's great. I know you can learn all of your lines. We'll work together next week, okay?"

"Okay!" She throws her arms around my legs, laughing.

Am I high? My head reels.

"There's my mom . . . see ya!" And she's gone.

"So will I grow, so live, so die," I whisper and burn rubber.

CHILDREN'S WRITES

Dear Diary,

Oberon wants to have my servent boy! I can't because I promised a human friend that died and I promised her I will take care of his son. Titania.

LESSON PLAN

When "teachers" acting on a television show complete a tough scene, the director calls "Cut!" The "teacher" has her hair and makeup retouched and is offered a refreshing drink while the charming actors playing her "kids" compliment her talent.

William is working late, so I throw together a salad and plant myself in front of the TV to catch up on the news. Iraq is in freefall as three warring cultures whip up civil unrest. The Middle East is exploding in enmity. A hornet's nest of hate.

Hate can't be reasoned with. Hate is a hungry monster demanding nourishment. Intolerance of other human beings is something that is nurtured. The laying down of swords for peace is inconceivable by those filled with hate.

It can be exhilarating to seek power and revenge. Self-righteousness is a powerful drug. Hate is a quick high.

Compassion, empathy, and generosity may feel better, but they take effort.

Today, I was so angry at those kids. I couldn't find my power and wanted revenge. I was slipping to the dark side. This cannot be; it quite simply cannot be. I have to get a grip.

I can't get to the bottom of their grievances. I can't sort out their cliques and revenge scenarios. All I can do, one Shakespearean line at a time, is keep them on course to a greater prize.

"Once more unto the breach, dear friends, once more . . ."

CHAPTER XV

442 YEARS OLD

Speak you so gently? Pardon me, I pray you.
I thought that all things had been savage here,
And therefore put I on the countenance
Of stern command'ment.

As You Like It Act II, Scene VII

"Y ou may wonder why I wanted to create the Shakespeare Club."

No, they don't. Children don't really consider these sorts of things. I showed up in Room 15. They showed up in Room 15. Fact. *Why* isn't on their radar.

"Do you know what a reality show is?"

"Is *The Simpsons* a reality show?" Miles asks. He thinks Bart Simpson is a real person, which explains a lot.

"*The Simpsons* is not a reality show. Shows like *Survivor* and *American Idol* are reality shows."

"*You* watch *American Idol*?" Marin asks, incredulous.

"No, I don't."

"My mom won't let me watch *American Idol* or any of those shows," Dana offers.

"That's good, because your mom is saving you from a lot of crap TV—"

"Ms. Ryane!" Candace cries. "You can't say—"

"Got it, Candace. Settle down and listen to my point. All these television shows have one thing in common. There's a winner, there's lots of losers, and there's a great deal of meanness."

They pay attention because they like to hear about winners and losers.

"So, I'm doing Shakespeare Club because you guys are my very own reality show."

Marin balances back on two chair legs, looking exactly like a juvenile delinquent in some 1960s school drama. Candace repeatedly mouths the word *crap* to punish me.

"Every single one of you has what it takes to be that winner. You're all capable of reaching your full potential in life."

They're quiet, which is something, but they squint with a look that screams *bored*.

"Here's what I mean."

On the board:

1. A LIFE OF MEANING

"The fastest way to a meaningful life is to do stuff for people before they ask for help."

2. A LIFE OF ADVENTURE

"You can have a life of adventure when you travel. Until you have the money and freedom to get on a bus, train, or plane, the best way to travel is by reading books. You can go many places in books."

3. A LIFE OF PEACE

"I want you all to have a life of peace. I don't want you to worry about having food or paying your rent. So, finish at Arden Street, finish middle school, finish high school, go to college, and find a job you love. Everyone in this room has the ability to do that."

I let that sit. We study each other in silence, and I complete my pitch by holding up a journal.

"Last week, you ripped pages out of your journals and had a paper war. You wasted something that should have been precious to you."

Dana opens her mouth, catches my eye, and snaps her mouth shut.

Good choice.

"Only *one* of you used her time to journal write. As of this minute, she is the one person winning my reality show. She is the one person who will go the distance. The rest of you have to catch up because the bar has been set."

"What bar?" Carla asks.

"The imaginary bar that pushes you to jump higher than you thought possible."

"Ms. Ryane, you're talking funny again."

"Undoubtedly."

Oddly, the one who had set the bar was completely unaware of it. Anna, in her pink feather boa, had ignored the paper war and concentrated on her journal last week. Her entry was a criticism of her Titania. She didn't think she was "strong enough" as Titania and that she had to "be stronger and do better."

Anna is not a natural actor, but she is a kid who pushes herself to go further and do better. She has the courage to march to her own drummer. She dresses as she chooses, ignores the cliques, and fearlessly raises her hand to answer questions. Anna will be fine as she ventures into the world, but it won't always be a smooth ride. It's tough to be different.

"Do you mean you think we're losers?" Jennifer asks.

"No, you just aren't winners yet. You need to act like winners. Respect your work, your journals, your scripts, and respect the parts you're playing. Make sense?"

Marin ponders, Dana smolders, Jordan nods . . . and Carla twinkles. I'm not sure why, but Carla's putting a positive spin on this dressing-down from Ms. Ryane.

On the board:

> April 23, 1564
> April 23, 1616
> May 25

"Can anyone tell me why these dates are important?"

Anna's arm shoots high. "When William Shakespeare was born and when he died?"

"Exactly right. And how crazy is this: he was born and died on the same date. I wonder if he even opened his gifts before he died."

Jennifer waves. "Is the May one when we do the play?"

"Yup, that's the date we do the play—but only if we rehearse with focus and commitment. Can we do that?"

"We can do it," Regina declares.

"Regina seems to think we can do it. Anyone else have an opinion?"

"Yes, we can do it!" Carla yells.

The two most enthusiastic cast members are the two without speaking parts. I canvass the rest of them.

"I think we could do it," Marin murmurs.

"I don't," Miles pipes up.

"Anyone else?"

"Yes, we can," from Jordan, but nothing from her twin, Candace.

Dana is silent, but Stella says, "Yes, yes."

The votes are in, and the consensus is that we can do the play . . . unless Miles is psychic.

"But, Ms. Ryane." Jennifer has a worried look. "They're going to laugh at us."

"Jennifer, when the audience laughs, it'll be because something is funny. I guarantee you won't be laughed at just for being you. In fact, you'll be honored for doing this play."

"Right." Jennifer's tone is skeptical.

"Does everyone have the same fear Jennifer does?"

They nod vigorously.

I stare hard, burning a look into each of their little faces, and pace before them like Patton.

"Look at me straight in the eyes. I will *not* let that happen. I promise you I *will not* let that happen. Do the work, and you'll be respected."

Their doubt is robust, but it's all I can do for now. The rest will be their discovery.

"I have a little surprise for you," I say. "Because it's almost April 23, we're going to celebrate William Shakespeare's birthday with a party."

Screams rock the room.

"You mean we don't have to do no work?" Carla bubbles.

"Right, no work. Today, we're going to play games, eat pizza, drink juice, and have cupcakes in honor of William Shakespeare."

"Pizza!"

"Cupcakes!"

"Ms. Ryane, you're so cool!"

"It's true, thanks for noticing."

I'm a sucker for being called cool by the under-ten set. And so we party. We play hangman using names from *A Midsummer Night's Dream* and *Hamlet*. We play the telephone game. I whisper a phrase in somebody's ear, the sentence passes around the circle from ear to ear, and we listen to how it's changed.

"A green rabbit ate an orange carrot," I say to Grace, and I watch as one kid slips the line to another and another and—

"The bunny pooped!" Marin shouts from the end of the line. Here we go.

"The little girl in the pink dress danced for the queen." I send the missive off to ricochet around the group.

"The girl pooped in her dress!" Marin announces. Surprise.

I switch their seating and whisper, "The boy threw a ball at the wall."

"The boy pooped!" Regina shouts. Moving on.

Did Elizabethan children have an attraction to all things scatological? Is it biological that they find poop so killingly funny?

To foster further goodwill in Room 15, I concoct a game similar to the Shakespearean curses exercise we'd done months earlier. A paper bag is filled with note cards bearing the kids' names. Each child will pick a name from the bag, stand in front of that person, and compliment them.

Grace picks Miles. She moves to him with some reluctance.

"You have a blue shirt."

"That's a fact, not a compliment. Try again."

"You are sitting in a chair."

"Grace, come here."

She abandons a mortified Miles.

I pull Grace close. "A compliment is something nice about the person."

"I can't do that," she whispers back.

"Yes, you can, and I insist you do. Now go tell Miles he's doing a good job playing Lysander."

In front of Miles, she stares at the floor and mumbles, "You're a good Lysander."

"Oh, that's terrific, Grace," I loudly over-enthuse, clapping my hands. "And very true. Miles *is* doing a good job as Lysander."

Miles gives me a dry look. He's not buying it. They all struggle to say anything generous to each other. The lines in the sand have been drawn, and any hope of erasing them is a pipe dream.

Moving on.

"Before we continue on to the food portion of our party, I want you to open your journals. Remember when we wrote, 'If I can do Shakespeare, I can do anything'?"

Not really.

"Okay, stand up." I raise my hands for them to follow. "And, all together. . . ."

Nothing.

"And, all together: 'If I can—'"

"IF I CAN DO SHAKESPEARE, I CAN DO ANYTHING!"

"Rock on. Sure, Shakespeare's writing is hard to read and act, but if we can tackle his stuff, we can tackle anything. Believe me on this. Okay, outside."

They perch on a long bench, and I hand out individual pizzas I'd made at home along with juice boxes and cupcakes. Together, we munch in celebration of Shakespeare's birthday. Eating is the cohesive activity of the Shakespeare Club. There's peace, short-lived but real, as juice is slurped and frosting licked. In this community of consumption, innocence governs. I wish they'd feast on the play with as much gusto as the pizza.

Once they're gone, I pick up the empty juice boxes and cupcake wrappers. I gather journals and pencils in my roles as caterer and janitor of the Shakespeare Club. Crushing trash in my fist, I think: *This is what I can do. I can give them the play. I can lead them to the trough and encourage them to drink. I can set rules and boundaries, but the rest is up to them. This in itself is the painful aspect.* At the end of the day, I have no control over their choices.

CHILDREN'S WRITES

— *I want to be in the Shakespeare Club because my mom made me.*
— *I want to be in the Shakespeare club because it is going to give me courage my bravery in the future and help get a better job in the future.*

LESSON PLAN

Mistakes will be made.

Dana and I have engaged in a dance of terrible missteps across an icy surface. To smooth things out, I suggest we do some private work in the library.

"You have to call my mom and tell her because she won't believe me if I tell her I'm staying late to do that," she says. Not a big surprise.

"Okay, I can call your mom. Is the extra work something you'd like to do? You do have most of the lines in the play."

"Yes, Ms. Ryane, I'd like to do it."

"Then over the weekend, go through your script and circle every word you don't understand or don't know how to pronounce."

I call Dana's mom and get permission.

On Wednesday, both Dana and Marin show up to the library. I get Marin situated circling her tricky words while I dig in with Dana. We settle across from each other.

"Ms. Ryane, can I ask you a question?"

"Of course."

"Who was it that wrote in their journal that day?" She gives me an even look, fully expecting an answer.

"Not telling," I reply, "but we know who *didn't*, don't we?"

Deflated, she peers at her script and points out the words she's circled.

"Dana," I interrupt. "Can I ask you a question?"

"Okay." She sounds wary.

"What's your dream? What do you think you'd like to do with your life?"

"Oh, I want to be an actress and also a singer." She smiles.

"Then Shakespeare Club is a good idea for you. Let's work toward your dream by doing the very best with these roles."

And so we work, and it's good work. We discuss her speeches and intention, and Dana starts to make sense of her dual roles as Oberon and Theseus. We finish up with time to spare.

"Dana, while you wait for the bus, please go over everything we've done. Whisper your lines to yourself, and it'll really make a difference when we rehearse next."

Dana nods. I'm certain we've broken new ground in our relationship.

"Okay, Marin, you're up."

As Marin and I pore over her lines, I watch Dana wander about the library. She picks up stuffed animals and examines them. She pulls out books and looks at their pictures. She toys with items on the librarian's desk. She does anything and everything except study her script. I'm disappointed but stay mum.

When it's time for her to leave, I say, "Good work today, Dana. Try to find some time to go over this before next Thursday, okay?"

"Sure, okay." She smiles as she closes the door.

Marin zips up her backpack, and we leave together. She tells me about her violin program and an upcoming concert she's attending at UCLA.

"Marin, that's exciting. I want you to notice something when you're on the

UCLA campus."

"What's that?"

"Look around the walkways, the green lawns, and the big buildings. Take a moment to imagine yourself at school there."

I'm taking a chance she won't ask me the obvious questions. *Did you go there, Ms. Ryane? What college did you go to, Ms. Ryane?*

I didn't go anywhere. No college for Ms. Ryane.

I didn't even attend my high school graduation ceremony. I grabbed my diploma and bolted. Never wore the cap and gown. I was outta there.

At eighteen, I boarded an airplane for the first time in my life and flew three thousand miles across Canada to the beautiful and exotic city of Montreal. The plane ticket was an unexpected graduation gift from my parents.

In Montreal, my true love was waiting for me. Four years older than me, yet still very young, my boyfriend Brendan, the director of a theatre company, was on a national tour to audition actors. While he worked, I roamed cobblestone streets and gaped awestruck at stylish French-Canadian women. I felt I was about to enter my adulthood. In Montreal, I drank beer. In Montreal, I ate escargot. In Montreal, Brendan and I fought like an old married couple.

He was angry at me . . . over what, I don't know. And I never would know because he wouldn't talk about it. In a rage, he abandoned me in a smoky, dark bar loaded with wild Quebecois revolutionaries. A little drunk, I weaved through the streets of Montreal and found Brendan at the train station, where we boarded a train and wended our way back west, sometimes laughing, sometimes loving, sometimes ignoring each other. Too young, too fast, too stupid. There was no moving back home with my parents after this. I couldn't tell them I had failed. This was the path to the theatre and my life as an actor.

Dad had packed the car with my belongings: cardboard boxes stuffed with clothes, childhood books, and a teddy bear. The night was slick with autumn rain, the sound of slushy tires providing the soundtrack as he drove me to my new home. Dad glanced at his eighteen-year-old daughter, her pale face intermittently lit by the white glow of the streetlamps. Her hair, long, dark, and straight, was parted down the middle.

She was on her way to another life, a virtual bride without a wedding. She was moving with her boyfriend into a tiny apartment because she was in love with him, in love with acting and drama.

The tangy cocktail of youth.

Dad searched for the appropriate words. My poor parents. They knew they couldn't keep me and what a choice to let go . . . but they did, and they were right to do so.

"You know you can always come back," Dad said. "If you want to go to university, we can get the money."

"Yeah, Dad, thanks."

Never going back rattled around in my head along with the swishing of the Volvo's windshield wipers.

Heartbreaking as it might have been for my father, he must have understood my need to leave. My dad was a wanderer, a seeker of foreign lands. Once retired, he filled a small travel bag with a swimsuit, clean T-shirts, and a chess set. He'd find a beach in Bali, set up his board, and play chess by himself until a fellow loner would join him.

"Best way to meet people," Dad crowed.

Back in Canada, we received photos of Dad in some Indonesian home, holding the family baby in the company of grinning strangers. We would peer at these pictures, at this strange man we knew yet didn't know at all. He took these trips for months at a time. India, Mexico, Australia, China, Malaysia, Burma . . .

Now, frail with age, Dad can only journey in his head. He recently told me, "Mel, I can die a happy man because the best thing I ever did in my life was travel."

Not *marry your mother* or *have you kids*. The best thing was getting as far away from us as possible.

I got it. Dad bore the wanderlust of William Shakespeare. Some of us are just like that.

"*I* could go there?" Marin asks, her eyes wide.

I give her shoulder a squeeze. "Yes, Marin, there's a place for you there, a spot waiting. You can definitely go to that university."

She looks at the ground and back at me, and takes off. "Okay, Ms. Ryane. See ya!"

It's different now. The days of backpacking through Europe in order to complete your education are gone. If you want to run away with the circus, try to find one with pension and health benefits.

I watch Marin make tracks on the playground. Maybe I've planted a small seed. Let it take root and blossom. Let her be smarter than me.

Hard not to notice I'm worrying like a mom. I never wanted to be that.

CHAPTER XVI

HITTING THE WALL

Is this a dagger which I see before me,
The handle toward my hand?

Macbeth Act II, Scene I

I'm going to start today by telling you something personal."

Up they sit. This could be yummy, could be good.

"I have two major weaknesses. One: I don't like being lied to. Two: I don't like my time being wasted."

Boring. They fidget in their chairs.

"Here's the thing," I continue. "Last week, I stayed in this room an extra *half-hour* searching for the markers someone hid. The markers that no one except me is supposed to touch."

Accusation and blame buzz through the room. They shoot killer looks at each other. I wait for them to settle. We use Room 15 by the grace of the math coach, and I'm expected to leave it in tidy condition, not with tools missing.

"Whoever is responsible will come to me at some point today and tell me why they hid those markers."

The buzz grows. I raise my voice.

"That person, for telling the truth, will be justly rewarded."

The noise stops.

Did she say *rewarded*? We get something? What . . . what?

"Remember, don't lie to me and don't waste my time. Those things put me in a bad mood."

I fetch my script, and as I turn around, I'm circled by five children.

"Me, it was me!" Stella cries.

"No, I think it was me!" Carla tops her.

"I'm not sure!" Regina wails.

"Maybe I did it," Miles adds.

Ridiculous. They actually think someone will receive a present for confessing.

"This should be interesting." I look down at the quintet of confessors. "Since no one is going to lie to me, I'm curious how this will work."

"Okay!" Carla shouts. "I didn't do it." She returns to her chair. Stella follows in quick suit, as do Regina and Miles.

Marin has worry etched on her face.

"I'm sorry, Ms. Ryane," she says. "It was an accident. We heard you coming back and the markers spilled and we couldn't find the jar and they slipped under the paper and I'm sorry . . . it was an accident."

"Hmmm . . . fairly good, as confessions go. Come here."

And I give Marin a hug.

As she sits, the others jump all over her, demanding to know what she got.

"A hug," Marin says. "That's all."

They groan.

Did they imagine I'd slip her a five-spot?

"Onward and upward!" I say. "Let's begin because time is running out. Later, I have a surprise for you."

What, what, what?

"Not saying." I open my script. "We have much to do first. Let's do the Oberon/Titania argument and then move to Pyramus/Thisbe. Ready?"

Dana and Anna take their places at the center of the carpet. Anna is already off-book and really acting as Titania. Across from her, Dana bumbles along as if our work in the library never happened.

"You two, try the scene again. Dana, when you say, 'Thou shalt not from this grove till I torment thee for this injury,' I want you to really mean it. You're very angry at the fairy queen."

"Do you want me to yell at her?" Dana asks, hopeful.

"You don't necessarily have to yell. Sometimes, we get so furious we can only whisper, but you know what that kind of mad feels like. Give it a try."

They run the scene again, and Dana shrieks at Anna, "*WHY SHOULD TITANIA CROSS HER OBERON I DO BUT BEG A LITTLE CHANGELING BOY!*"

All the air has been sucked out of the room. We stare at Dana's hot, red face. Dana unleashed.

I clear my throat.

"Well, that was certainly a direction to consider, and we'll visit this scene again. Let's move on to the play within a play."

Dana primly takes her seat, unaware of the wide berth her fellow actors give her.

"I need six jolly men."

Stella, Marin, Candace, Jordan, and Carla crawl on all fours to the center of the carpet, but I'm short one jolly man. Originally, it was Azra, then Dana, but the former has disappeared, and the latter is a far cry from jolly.

"Carla, you play Tom Snout, and Stella, you be Snug, the joiner. Regina, if I beg you on hand and knee, could you try Robin Starveling?"

The three girls rifle through their scripts. Carla will have one speech, Regina a smaller one, and Stella will roar as the lion. Thrilled, Stella shows off her fantastic ability to roar. It beats whining.

Regina silently mouths her speech. I await her decision.

"Ms. Ryane, how will I do this? The moon. How can I be a moon?" she asks.

"In the Shakespeare Club box, I have a blue candle holder to use as a lantern. That's how Robin Starveling plays the moon."

"Oh . . . then I think I could do this." She smiles.

"Terrific, Regina, you'll be great as the moon. Well, Carla, what do you think?"

"Okay, I'll do this Tom Snout," she says, and purses her lips.

We start the play within the play. Candace remains dark and moody, and I want to kick her out of the club. No amount of cupcakes, hugs, or encouragement has knocked Candace or Dana off the ship of blues. Our comedy is dry of comedy.

Until Carla arrives center stage, ready to play a character who plays . . . a wall. This is remarkable, considering the group is full of girls who want to be fairies. A wall falls somewhat below fairies on the glamour scale.

Candace, at Carla's feet, sullenly ekes out her words.

BOTTOM
Thou wall, O wall, O sweet and lovely wall
Show me thy chink, to blink through with mine eyne.

Carla crams her script under one armpit, reaches out her right arm, and opens two fingers into a V to create a hole. She's adorable and funny and checks in with me to see if this is okay. *Yes, yes,* I nod.

BOTTOM
> *Thanks, courteous wall. But what see I?*
> *No Thisby do I see.*

Candace is barely audible, and I could strangle her. Try, for God's sake, *try.* Marin, as Thisbe, steps to Carla's other side. Carla reaches her left arm out and opens two fingers into another V. Carla's inventiveness is making me laugh.

FLUTE
> *O wall, my cherry lips have often kissed thy stones.*

Carla cocks her head, sports a dry look, and contemplates being kissed by Marin. Carla's naturally comedic and has lifted our spirits. She inspires Regina to hold her lantern high while belting out her speech.

STARVELING
> *This lantern doth the moon present*
> *Myself the man in the moon seem to be.*

"Carla and Regina, you've impressed me. You stepped up to the plate. Really good, thank you, girls," I say, and check my script to see where we should go next.

I glance up and see my compliment to "the little kids" is a dagger lodged in Dana's gut. Half-lidded, she glowers at them, then at me.

What makes a person want to act? To take action? To stand before an audience and lay bare the sadness, rage, and tenderness that most of us hold inside and care not to sell on the open market?

At three years of age, I took to the stage by way of a stranger's doorstep. It was Halloween. This holiday would come to define my mother's zest and zeal for costuming. On my first Halloween, she sent me out as a potato.

Food products were popular costumes at the time. The Sears catalogue had pages of people dressed as hot dogs, tomatoes, and celery. A potato fit right in and could be pulled together rather cheaply. Mom put me in a brown cardigan and brown tights, then added a brown jumper with a brown hood she had sewn. Holes were cut for my eyes, nose, and mouth.

I clutched my dad's hand as he led us through the dark neighborhood on a foggy night. Big kids ran screaming past. The air was spiced with the smoky smell of spent fireworks. This was an adventure, and I was protected by both my hood and my Dad.

Until the door. The door was gigantic. Dad released my hand and gently steered me forward to knock and recite my line. I made a fist and pounded the door. It opened, and light poured over me.

I was on.

"Trick or treat!" I said in as loud a voice as I could muster.

A couple looked down at me. They smiled. They crouched down.

"Well, look here . . . what are you, honey?" the missus asked.

"Oh, isn't that something," added the mister. "You must be a . . . a . . . well, to be honest, I'm not sure."

"A potato!" I said, holding out my paper bag as rehearsed.

"Ahhh, of course, that's it. I see it now," he said, dropping a piece of candy in the bag.

The missus looked sour as she whispered to her husband, "Jack, she looks like a little turd. What a terrible thing to do to a child."

"No," I said, "I'm a *potato*."

Is this a seed that can make a person want to act? Revenge? Proof? Thrust headfirst into the limelight, acting my way out of a silly costume? Perhaps.

I can help an actor make choices in a scene. I can teach the craft, the technique. But no one can *make* a person act. No one can give the gift of timing, or the insatiable curiosity to know why humans do what we do to get what we want, and no one can make the emotional instrument accessible.

The need to act is heaven's curse, and when you have the hunger, there's not much to be done but sell it. Out front and center.

———

Dana makes me crazy because she has an actor's instrument. I see it. Her emotions sit high, ready, and on alert. Now I want her to embrace discipline. I want her to discover that her rage has a place. There's a home for all that feeling, but she's trapped inside a potato costume.

"Dana, are you ready to continue?" I'm determined to ignore her disdain.

Dana shuffles into place, arms folded over her chest, as she shifts her weight to one hip. She's a dark cloud hovering over the sun. Her mood infects the room.

We meander our way cheerlessly to the end of the play. Dana mutters her lines, Candace scowls, and once again, our play is hardly recognizable as a comedy. In a scant few weeks, they're supposed to perform, and we've only just now finished staging the damn thing.

"Congratulations, we made it to the end. Now, your surprise."

I hold up a bright orange sheet of paper. It's an invitation to a "staged reading" of *A Midsummer Night's Dream* with a date, their names, and the roles they're playing.

Nervous and hyper, they press forward to see their names.

"Oh, Ms. Ryane, I'm so scared!"

"What if people don't come?"

"What if too many people come?"

"What if *kids* come?"

"No kids, Ms. Ryane, make a rule that no kids can come . . . please, please?"

"But, my cousins have to come, and they're kids!"

"No, please! Don't let Jennifer's other cousins come, please, Ms. Ryane, make a rule!"

"Here's how this is going to go," I say. "Each of you will get four invitations to invite whoever you would like."

I made the orange program as an incentive to promote discipline in our rehearsals, and it worked. I start to get requests for private coaching. They're lining up to meet with me.

"Ms. Ryane?"

"Yes, Candace?"

"Could I practice with you on Tuesday?"

"Of course. See you at two-thirty in the library."

For the first time in weeks, Candace smiles.

"Dana?"

I catch her at the door. She lumbers toward me. Her look sends a drafty chill my way.

"I think your focus is misplaced." I put my hand on her shoulder. "Dana, you didn't do the follow-up I suggested. Today, you fumbled around in rehearsal. You're better than that. You can do these roles, but you give your attention to other people instead of your own work."

Her eyes darken. No one likes being busted, but for Dana, this signals a blood battle. Taciturn, she spins away. I consider myself warned.

Miles is standing in the doorway. As Dana passes, she brazenly leads with her shoulder and slams him into the frame. She doesn't care that I've seen this. Miles is unfazed.

"Lysander, as I live and breathe," I volunteer, hoping to take the sting out of Dana's cruelty.

"Well, maybe I could . . . you know . . . work with you . . . you know . . . on my part . . . you know . . . in the library," Miles murmurs.

I slouch against the doorframe and give him a serious look.

"You think I should take another chance on your showing up? You've stood me up *three* times, Miles. Why would I believe you this time?"

He studies the floor and sweeps it with his heavy backpack. Back and forth, he drags it. He looks up, he looks down.

"Well . . . because I'll come . . . that's why."

"All right, Wednesday, Miles. In the library at two-thirty. Be there. I'm not kidding."

He nods and starts to leave.

"Miles."

He turns back.

"What day is today?"

"Um . . . Thursday?"

"That's right, it's Thursday. Can you remember Wednesday? Because I'm not going to track you down every day to remind you."

"Yeah. See ya, Ms. Ryane."

I'm almost finished cleaning up when Candace arrives, breathless.

"Nick Bottom, lovely to see you." But not really because her face says something's up. All of a sudden, I'd like to be in my car en route to a chilled Pinot Gris.

"Ms. Ryane! I have something to tell you . . . a message, kind of . . . and I want you to know this isn't what I would ever say to you—not me—I wouldn't—it's just a message."

Great.

"What is it, Candace?" I make my voice as bored as possible.

"But you have to know *I* wouldn't ever say this to you. It's from Dana . . . she said to say this, not me." Candace is near frantic.

"Okay, Candace, I believe you. Now, what is it?"

She holds a script out to me.

"This is Dana's," Candace says.

"And?" I take the script and wait.

"She quit Shakespeare Club and said for me to give this to you and to tell you—really, Ms. Ryane—I would never say this to you . . . she said to *throw* it in your face and . . ."

"Go on."

" . . . to tell you . . . to go to hell."

Candace lets out a long, sad sigh and shakes her head, her eyes glued to me for a reaction.

"So, Candace."

"Yeah?"

"It seems Dana is pretty unhappy."

"Yeah."

"Let's find a way not to be like that, okay?" I give Candace a hug. "Let's start by working together next week on Nick Bottom." I lift her chin and look into her eyes. "Deal?"

"Yeah!" She smiles and walks away, then stops.

"I wouldn't, you know, say that."

"I know. See you next week." I give her a wave.

How prescient of the young Dana. I'm already in hell.

CHILDREN'S WRITES

Dear Diary,
Francis Flute doesn't want to play a girls part, so he is not happy with what he has.

LESSON PLAN

Not every principal, teacher, parent, or child will agree that your ideas are workable, interesting, or beneficial.

At home, I whip up a Caesar salad and top it with freshly grilled salmon. I pour the wine and sit across from William.

"How did it go today?" he asks.

"Oh, fabulous."

"Really?"

"A fifth-grader told me to go to hell." I sip my wine.

"I hear hell has good food."

"It makes up for a lot." I smile. "As does the company."

On Wednesday, in the library, I check my watch and peer out the blinds. I'm giving Miles exactly three minutes to show. Outside, kids wander to yellow buses, kick soccer balls, and chat in groups. No Miles among them.

I sigh and watch as the clock reaches 2:33. I gather my script and my bag and turn toward the door—

Where he stands, still and quiet, his heavy backpack on the floor next to him. How long has he been there?

Miles, Miles, Miles.

I try to suppress a smile, but it's too late. His own delight springs forth in a wide grin. He knows I'm surprised to see him. Something in Miles knows he has a gift.

"Take a seat, my friend."

Miles places his script on the table and accepts the pencil I offer him.

"Before we start, I'd like to ask you something."

He nods.

"What do you think about being in Shakespeare Club? I mean, if you were asked by another kid if being in the club was a good idea, what would you say?"

He takes a long moment before answering. With the pencil, he stabs at the cover of his script, leaving a trail of tiny dots.

"Well, I would say it's a good thing, but we need more boys. I was kinda shy at the start and now I'm better, but with more boys, I wouldn't be so shy and it would be better."

Shy is not a word I would use to describe Miles, but it's his word, and I respect that.

"I suggest you and I together try to recruit more boys for the club. You talk to them and let them know it can be fun, and I'll do the same."

"Okay."

"Let's work on Lysander."

Miles and I work for forty minutes. We go through all his speeches from top to bottom. He's clear and animated in a way I haven't seen in rehearsal.

"Miles, what do you think of Lysander?"

"He's brave. He goes in the forest and he runs away and he's brave."

"Are you like Lysander?"

"I want to be brave like him."

"Do you know what makes this day different from all the other days we were supposed to meet and you didn't show up?"

He shrugs.

"You made a choice to be here, that's all. Remember the stick and the two rocks? Remember how I made you make a choice that day?"

He nods as he stabs more dots into his script.

"Today, you made a brave choice."

He stops, lays down his pencil, and nods.

"*King Kong!*" Dana screams at me. "That's what he called me, King Kong!"

Mystery solved. This was Miles's silver bullet shot into Dana's heart. The missive I'd sensed and missed weeks ago.

I'd found Dana during lunch break. "Dana, is it true you want to quit Shakespeare Club?"

She'd stomped around in a circle. I'd followed behind and listened to her unload.

"And you did nothing—*nothing!*—about it!"

She skids to a stop and turns on me.

"You let them get away with everything! You never tell the little kids any-thing!" She lunges off, leaving me in her wake.

I stop and wait for her to exhaust herself. Tears stream down her cheeks and snot from her nose. I hand her a tissue and suggest we sit on a bench. Reluctantly, she complies, making sure there's a good five feet between us.

"That was a horrible thing for him to say. I'm so sorry that happened."

She shakes her head, furious.

"Dana, I'm just wondering. Have you ever insulted anyone in Shakespeare Club? Have you ever called anyone any names?"

"No! They do it, the little kids!"

"I want you to think about my question again, and remember my two weak points. I don't take well to being lied to or my time being wasted."

She's in my face now. "I didn't throw that paper, and I didn't say bad things!"

"Like I said, lying doesn't sit well with me, and that's what you're doing. I know you've called the others names because I've heard you, and I'm not even going to discuss the paper war again. *Saying* something is true doesn't *make* it true."

"But you're not fair," she hisses.

"It may seem that way, but you don't hear all the private conversations I have with everyone in the group. So you don't really know. Unfortunately for you and every kid in school, name-calling, gossip, and meanness are an awful part of the playground experience."

Dana frowns and kicks a pebble.

"It happens to everyone, not just you. It happened to me when I was your age." She squints at me.

"It's just the way it is, and I'm not going to get in the middle of it. If I do, all the Shakespeare Club time will be spent with me sorting out nastiness, and we'll never get anything done. We'll never rehearse, and we'll never, ever be able to do a performance."

"But . . . it's not fair—"

"Give it up, Dana. Stay with the big picture. You want to be an actress, right?"

"Yes."

"Being an actress means you have to be strong and accept lots of stuff that isn't fair and nice. It's all about rejection. What do you think happens when lots of actors audition for a part, and only one person gets it?"

Dana turns her back to me.

"You have a chance, right here and now, to rise with the strength inside you or to give into weakness."

She glances back, brow knitted as she wrestles with my argument. I get up, take her shoulders, and look her straight in the face.

"Dana, don't give in to weakness. Work on your script and rise above this because if you don't, they win. So what if you were called a name? So what? Don't call anyone else names, and if it happens to you, get taller, not smaller."

I drop to the bench, the distance between us a little less wide. We sit in silence for a few minutes until the bell rings

"Am I going to see you on Thursday?" I ask.

"I guess." She rises to leave.

As she shambles away, I call, "Dana, if you quit, you'll let everyone down. We can't do the play without you. You have two huge parts."

She freezes, her back to me, and I suppose she might be contemplating.

"Can I give you a hug?" I ask as I get up.

She nods, and I put my arms around her. "It'll be okay, you'll see. You're going to start having fun now, okay?"

"I have to go now." I watch her amble to class.

That went well, I think, giving myself a pat on the back.

There's a woman in India—a guru, I suppose—known as "The Hugging Saint." She travels the world hugging people and by doing so, changes lives for the better.

It turns out I'm not that woman.

I'd unsuspectingly slipped Dana the ammunition she needed. A young girl longing for recognition, status, and affection was left unsatisfied and thus, as Shakespeare would have observed, she'd located a road to power and revenge.

Dana had forgotten the lesson on irony. She didn't know she was already playing Oberon. Angry and hurt, Oberon hungers for adoration. Bereft, he seeks revenge by making Titania fall in love with a donkey.

"We can't do the play without you."

That's all Dana needed to hear, and that's all I heard a couple of days later.

"Dana quit!"

"Who's going to play Oberon?"

"Who's going be Theseus?"

The spoils of war are once more up for grabs. I sigh and grapple with if we can still do this play.

I want to say, "Bottom's not the ass. You're lookin' at her."

Battles for power, revenge, and love. You'll find them in any schoolyard.

CHAPTER XVII

WHAT FOOL THIS MORTAL BE

I do now remember a saying,
"The fool doth think he is wise, but the wise man knows himself to be a fool."

As You Like It Act V, Scene I

I can't do the play because my mom says we have to be in Colorado on the day we're supposed to do it . . . so could you change the date, then I could do it? But not if you don't."

"Thanks, Dana, for telling me this, but no, we're not changing the performance date."

"Then I can't do it." She stares at me with arms crossed.

"It was nice knowing you, Dana. We're going to rehearse now. Bye."

I feel horribly cruel and instantly ashamed of myself, but I'm so pissed off. I don't believe her story.

I call Dana's mother.

"Yes, what is this regarding?" The iciness in her voice is undeniable.

"Dana tells me you're going to be out of town for our performance date. Is this true?"

"Yes, it is," she answers, sharp.

"That's unfortunate. Dana's worked hard on her roles and—"

"It *is* too bad," she cuts me off, "but it can't be helped." *Click.*

Her family may indeed be on its way out of town, but had Dana really wanted to perform and not felt ganged up on, I'm sure we wouldn't be in this mess.

I find Mr. Davis, Dana's fifth-grade teacher. Mr. Davis is a robust fellow with a few extra pounds bulging over the waistband of his jeans. I read his profile on the school website. He's a Navy vet, and it shows in how he manages his students. I envy his ability to negotiate order in his classroom. He uses a gruff, surly tone devoid of sentiment, and it seems to work. I thought I'd get some straight talk from Mr. Davis.

"Yup, Dana mentioned she was having trouble in the Shakespeare Club. Dana's a highly sensitive girl, but I get along very well with both her and her mother. They like me." I recall Dana's story of Mr. Davis kicking her out of student council and chorus. It seems everyone has recovered and moved on.

"I told Dana you'd have trouble managing a group of kids and that she should cut you some slack. I told her you aren't a *real* teacher."

This is a little more straight talk than I had in mind. I pull the dagger from my stomach and silently call Mr. Davis a bad name.

Let me be clear: Mr. Davis isn't wrong in his evaluation of my shortcomings. But he was very wrong in sharing his opinion with a student, infecting the playground with teacher politics. He tipped his hand. He sounds competitive.

The gifted American playwright, Alfred Uhry, wrote a play, *Without Walls*. The central character is a drama teacher in New York City in the 1970s. The story tells of a compelling triangle between the teacher and two of his students.

At the end of the play, the student who has become a professional actor throws a barrelful of frustration at his former teacher. Crushed that his teacher hasn't come to see his performances, the young actor attacks him. "We were friends, man!"

The teacher, equally dismayed by circumstances that have led to the end of his career, quietly states, "We were never friends. We were needy."

I was startled by the clean, bare truth of that line. The dance between a teacher and student has to be micromanaged by the adult. It's a high-wire act because none of us are free from being needy. Both kids and adults want attention and acknowledgment.

Perhaps Dana's mother, tired of listening to her daughter's complaints, told her to quit. Perhaps Mr. Davis, wanting to be the favored teacher, shared more than was ethical. Perhaps I failed Dana because I couldn't let her go. I'd refused to honor her choice to screw up and leave. Her departure sealed one more notch on my belt of failure.

Three adults conspired to prop up Dana's weak side and not demand her strength. Three adults in competition over this young girl's affection failed to give her the direction she needed.

Disconsolate, I wonder if there's any way I can salvage the situation. I can't let it be. Meanwhile, back in Room 15, I have the stupefying task of spreading my last ten thespians across even more roles.

"Candace, I think you should play Duke Theseus, and Jordan, you're going to play Oberon." The sisters clap their hands, completely clueless about how much work they've just inherited.

Jordan will come close to conversing with herself by playing four characters. She'll run, scurry back and forth, drop a sword, pick up a crown, flip a clipboard, and don a fairy wreath like a crazed vaudevillian. Candace's chores will be slightly more manageable once she conjures up the necessary courage to play the uproarious Bottom.

"Candace, you're going to have to be braver than you ever thought possible," I say as we launch into rehearsal. "When Nick Bottom becomes the donkey and sings for Titania, he believes he has a fantastic voice. He's proud of himself. Titania thinks he's brilliant because she's under a spell."

Candace's knuckles are white as she holds tight to her chair.

"Stretch your arms, Candace, and from the top of your lungs let those *hee haws* ring."

She releases her grip and drops her face into her hands.

"I promise that if you give this one hundred percent, it'll work and you'll be a hit. But if you only do it a little bit, it'll fall flat and feel terrible. Trust me on this."

She shakes her head back and forth and won't meet my eyes. I gently pry one hand from her face.

"Look, Candace. We'll do it together."

I settle myself and reach my arms wide to the sky. I close my eyes as if I'm about to belt out a barn-burner from *Gypsy*.

"Hee haw, hee haw, hee haw!"

Skeptical, Candace watches me.

"Sometimes, acting is just being an idiot in front of people," I tell her. "Believe me, I've had plenty of practice."

She looks like she's deciding whether this acting stuff is for her.

I proffer my hands, and she takes a light hold. The room is quiet as the rest of the kids witness courage in the making.

Again I give a lusty calling—"*Hee haw! Hee haw!*"—keeping my eyes locked on hers.

We circle in a slow dance, and she starts to join me. Faint at first, she gradually finds some volume.

"Hee haw!"

"That's right! Again!"

"Hee haw!"

We twirl in a circle.

"Hee haw! Hee haw!"

Louder and louder until we're spinning. I release her hands, and with full force, she takes off as Nick Bottom the donkey.

"*Hee haw! Hee haw! Hee haw!*"

Candace could have been on a bike, on an ice rink, or on a high board. Baby steps and here she is. An actor.

The other kids are laughing and clapping at Candace's giddy performance.

I lead Anna to the center of the floor to be Titania near her donkey.

TITANIA
What angel wakes me from my flow'ry bed? I pray thee, gentle mortal, sing again.

BOTTOM
Hee haw, hee haw, hee haw—

Candace is wickedly funny, brave, and proud of herself. I leap up, applauding.

Yes, kids, you are making history. Candace has found the confidence she needs to be an ass in front of the most critical of audiences, her own peers.

From that day forward, Candace will play Nick Bottom as the quintessential fool he is meant to be. She never wavers, and she reaps the benefits, justly deserved.

As one goes up, many bounce down on this teeter-totter called the Shakespeare Club. We have exactly two more rehearsals until May 25. It's impossible for me to imagine it.

On the board: RUN-THROUGH!

"We have so little time to polish up our play," I say. They squirm in their seats. "I want you to remember *you'll* be up there in front of the audience. I won't be doing this for you. You'll be doing it."

"Where will you be?" Stella demands.

"I'll be nearby, watching and following along in case you need help, but I won't be up there with you."

Miles sports a glum look, as if this is brand-new information.

"What happens to eggs in a bird's nest?" I ask.

"The babies hatch?"

"And what does Mama bird do?"

"She feeds them?"

"Then what?"

Silence.

"She tosses them out of the nest. It's time for you to fly. I'm giving you *kid power*. You'll be up there all by yourselves, flying. Grown-ups are going to have to sit up, be still, and listen to you. This will be your time—not mine, not your parents', not your teachers'."

They shrug.

Maybe they'll discover this on the day. I don't want to be one of those worry-wart adults calling out cues in a panic, one of those bleacher coaches who freaks out at a misplay. They'll depend on each other and learn more from mistakes than successes. They have a right to that.

"Here we go! Ready . . . and action, Marin!"

We get through page one, and it all falls apart. Regina reads the chorus alone. Stella fools around with her fairy headdress. She puts it on backward, which makes Carla laugh. Miles pokes Grace with his sword, Jennifer drifts asleep, Jordan, suddenly moody, has her back to the rest, and Candace doodles on her script.

"Stop. I'm curious why Regina is the only actor doing the chorus. *Chorus* means everybody . . . all of you . . . anyone who isn't onstage playing a part reads the chorus."

They fidget.

"Let's pick it up at Hermia's entrance." The charm of playing Hermia has abandoned Stella. She remains in her chair and ignores her cue.

"Stella?"

She looks up, blank.

"Are you playing Hermia?"

"Yeah."

"Are you playing Hermia today?"

"Oh, okay."

We're underwater, in quicksand. We're anywhere but here in this room having a run-through.

"You have exactly two more rehearsals before you perform. It seems like you want to ignore this one. What can I say to get you to focus? I'm at a loss."

They look at me as if I'm speaking German.

"Do you guys even like this play?"

"I love this play!" Stella exclaims, "but we should have costumes . . . then I would love it more!"

"I sympathize, but we don't have costumes. We have props, we have parts, and we have a great story to tell. These are the tools of our magic."

That's the problem? They want costumes?

After three more attempts to resuscitate the run-through, I call it. I'm done, finished, burnt. The kids are hitting and kicking each other. They whisper, snort, and giggle.

"Remember my weak points? Like my time being wasted?" My voice is soft and crackly, and for a second, I have their attention. "Today would be a good example of that. I don't think you want to rehearse today. You've made that clear. So we won't rehearse today."

"Then what will we do?" Jennifer asks.

"I'm going home. I suggest you call your parents to pick you up, or meet up with another after-school program, or go play on the playground because Room 15 is closed for the day."

I pack the props. The room is very, very still.

I glance over my shoulder at big eyes and mouths hanging wide enough to show missing teeth.

"Really, you can go now. I'll see you here next Thursday. Bye!" Light and friendly.

"But . . . but, Ms. Ryane," Regina whimpers. "We want to do Shakespeare Club."

"I don't think so, Regina. We tried four times to start a run-through, but no one wants to work. You have the rest of the day off."

The speed exhibited by Miles would interest NASA. He snatches his backpack and slams out the door. Jordan and Candace are quick to follow. Anna takes her time. Marin and Jennifer stroll out together.

Four stay behind. The ones Dana called "the little kids."

"Get your stuff. You can go."

Regina, Grace, Stella, and Carla are grouped together and stare at me.

"Please, Ms. Ryane," Stella says, "can't we please do Shakespeare Club?"

"Stella, you were one of the worst today, and now you want to rehearse?"

Stella studies her shoes.

"I know but please . . . anyway?"

I feel my hard-ass stance melting.

"I'll consider having a run-through, but you guys have to agree as a group to work hard and make it happen. Go and talk to the other members. I'll wait to see if you can get everyone back."

They take off. I peep out the window as they huddle up and take a meeting. Miles joins the girls. Within minutes, they're back inside.

Except one.

"Jordan won't come back," Jennifer says.

"Why?"

"She says she quits," Candace informs me. "She's in after-school on the other side." She points across the schoolyard.

I'm stuck. My threat almost worked, but we can't do a run-through with a partial cast.

"Okay, set the chairs up, get your scripts, and prepare your props. I will return."

I exit the room, purposely leaving my car keys behind so I'm not tempted to make a run for it. I stride to the far play area with fake confidence. What am I supposed to say? And why Jordan, of all of them? She has four roles to play.

I turn the corner and find her lounging at a picnic table, yukking it up with a group of kids I don't recognize. I flash back to this very same scene I played with Daniel months previous.

"Jordan" is all I'm able to muster.

She shoots me the sardonic gaze of someone who holds all the cards. Because I've already been in this position twice, I'm weakened. Daniel and Dana have undercut me. I don't know how to argue this anymore. I don't even know what the argument is anymore.

"Jordanna." I use her full name to signal that we're in a serious conversation. "Are you leaving Shakespeare Club?"

"Yeah." She's sure of herself, and I'm envious.

"But . . . why?"

"Just don't want to do it anymore." Clipped.

I have nothing to say. I shake my head. My mouth opens and closes.

I just lost to a ten-year-old girl.

This is it. It's over, ended. Without Jordan playing her multiple characters, we can't do a "staged reading" or whatever the hell I thought we could do. It's finished, and I have to go back to Room 15 and tell the others I've lost the battle and that I'm not the leader they thought I was.

In truth, I'd been fantasizing about this. The moment when I could walk away from the Shakespeare Club. But this isn't how it's supposed to feel. There's no relief. It's like a crumbling love affair; you know it's doomed but hang on anyway until you're dumped.

I've been dumped.

Jordan has turned from me and is jabbering to her new buddies, free and frivolous. When I see that, a current shoots up my spine, and I bolt my head into position as if an invisible string has yanked my puppet body into action.

"Jordan." I'm all business. "You can do whatever you'd like, but first, you have to come back to collect your journal and script."

"Sure," she says, and pops up.

Sometimes old and crafty wins the race.

Okay. She's following me as I return to Room 15. Time to beg. I'm not proud anymore.

Abruptly, I brake. Jordan breezes past me.

"Don't!" I shout.

Jordan spins around.

"Don't do it. Don't quit."

She doesn't speak. She stares and waits.

"This isn't what you want to do, Jordan. If you leave Shakespeare Club, you're giving yourself permission to be a quitter, always."

Neither of us moves as I gather steam.

"If you quit today, you're telling yourself it's okay to quit in sixth grade and then in twelfth grade and in college and always and forever. You'll know you're a quitter, Jordan, and that's not who you are."

She doesn't appear to be breathing. Two tears are trailing down her face. I take a small step forward, as if nearing an injured animal.

"What is it, Jordan?"

"The little kids . . . you let the little kids . . ."

Stop me if you've heard this before.

"Jordan, those aren't even your words. You've picked them up from someone else. Maybe you're mad at me for something, and that's okay, but you won't hurt me by quitting. You'll only hurt yourself."

Her tears are flowing fast. I dig in my pocket for a tissue.

"Blow." She does. I give her an even look.

"You'll have the best time of your life when we do the play. Do you believe me?"

Jordan nods. I'm so grateful I almost need the soggy tissue myself. We share a smile and silently make a pact.

Behind us, I can hear raucous screams from Room 15. I left them alone long enough to disintegrate into complete chaos . . . but it was worth it to get Jordan back.

Arm in arm, Jordan and I enter Room 15—and I lose it when I see the kids congregated around the whiteboard, markers flying everywhere.

"Oh, *come on*! You say you want to be disciplined and then you break more rules! Who did this? Who took the markers and did this?"

The room is quiet as I glare at them. No one breathes.

Then I look up.

On the board:

WE ARE SORRY, MS. RYANE!!!

Hearts and stars and fairies surround the letters. Someone's started a picture of a donkey.

Chagrined, I look back at them, mouth agape. They're pleased to have fooled me.

"And then you make Ms. Ryane cry. That's got to be another broken rule."

I smile and relax for the first time that day.

"Ready? Let's rehearse."

Jordan isn't up to snuff, mumbles her lines, and won't connect with the others. But she's with us.

And for the first time, we make our way through the play from beginning to end. Marin stands tall and speaks clearly. Miles is able to keep his sword sheathed until it's needed. Stella hits her marks, and the fairies sing to their queen as she slumbers next to a donkey.

We leave with a new sense of possibility. We're a group of ten and maybe we can stay ten and maybe I won't give myself permission to quit.

Flushed with having coaxed a lamb back to the flock, I hope my exuberance can erase the pain I'd experienced with Dana.

What fools these mortals be.

CHILDREN'S WRITES

The meaning of lonely is being somewere without people talking to you, not being with you, and most of the time when you are lonely you are sad.

LESSON PLAN

Teaching is a combat sport. Learning is even more brutal.

On Tuesday, Carla runs into the library, out of breath and excited to tell me something.

"Ms. Ryane—Ms. Ryane—I know it!" She beams.

"Okay, Carla, go for it."

She takes a breath and . . . and . . . and . . . it tumbles out.

WALL
In this play it doth befall,
That I, one Snout by name, present a wall.

And then:

WALL
Thus have I my part discharged so;
And, being done, thus Wall away doth go.

"Carla, magnificent. You've worked hard, and I'm proud of you. You didn't even want to read aloud when you started Shakespeare Club, and now you're playing a part and you know it by heart! On Thursday at rehearsal, I'll have a surprise for you."

"What is it?"

"It wouldn't be a surprise if I told you, would it?"

"Just for me? No one else?" Her eyes are big.

"Just for you." I watch her run off.

Carla is my reward for not quitting.

For a few weeks, I've noticed Dana at lunch or on the grounds. She has been pointedly avoiding me. As this continues, I fight an urge to glare at her. I have to remind myself I'm the adult in this relationship.

I come up with a plan and corner Dana.

"Dana, I know you're angry with me."

She nods rigorously and starts to speak, but I hold up my hand.

"And that's okay. It's all right that you're angry with me. You think I wasn't fair, and your argument is just fine."

Tears fill her eyes and she nods harder. Damn, she's a good crier.

"I think, even though you're upset, you miss Shakespeare Club."

"But I can't do it because—"

"I know you have plans with your family, but I have another suggestion. We have one rehearsal left, and I could use an assistant. I could use someone like you beside me to do a few helpful things."

"Like what?" She perks up.

"You could follow along in the script and help the actors when they get stuck. You could also videotape parts of the rehearsal so we have a record. I know you can use a camera."

"Yeah." She nods, agreeable.

"You could also help me get the props together and set up the room. You know, stuff like that. You could be back with the group, and you wouldn't have to carry around these sad feelings. What do you think?"

"I could do that, but you have to call my mom."

"You know what, Dana, I'm not going to call your mom. If you want to do this, you talk to her. She might be proud of you for not letting your bad feelings get in the way."

"Okay."

"'Okay, I want to help you' or 'okay, I want to think about it'? I'll be in the library on Wednesday, and you can let me know."

"Okay."

As she stood, I had a final thought.

"Dana, let's keep this between us, all right? The other kids won't be used to you as my helper, so if you do this, I'll introduce you as my assistant at the next meeting. Can you do that?"

"Sure." She nods.

"Hug?"

Dana kind of, sort of, almost does that.

Satisfied, I drive home to regale William with a tale of the détente I have skillfully negotiated on a lovely May afternoon. In a celebratory mood, I pour us glasses of red and grill pork chops and steam asparagus. William delights in my buoyancy as he cuts into the meal. I chatter on about how my Dana tactic would heal wounds and how I envisioned frothy happiness finally spilling out of Room 15 and how—

I stop. Both my fork and jaw hang in mid-air.

I'd done it again. I'd handed Dana another grenade.

We were never friends. We were needy.

Chapter XVIII

CRYIN' BAD

Yet let me weep for such a feeling loss.
Romeo and Juliet Act III, Scene V

Ms. Ryane! Ms. Ryane!"

The voices charge at me from across the schoolyard as I open Room 15.

God help me, here we go, here comes the grief. Since our conversation, Dana has avoided me. She's taken a pass on my olive branch and has chosen instead to spread terror among my young Shakespeareans.

Regina arrives first, followed by Grace and Carla. The little girls talk over each other, words bubbling and tumbling from their mouths.

"Girls. What's the news from the front?"

"Ms. Ryane, Dana says now *she's* the director of Shakespeare Club—"

"And *she* can boss us around and make us do what *she* wants—"

"And *you* told her *she* could tell us what to do and *she* can be as *mean* as she wants and she'll only be *nice* to the *big* kids and—"

"She'll *punish* us if we don't do what she says—"

I flatten my palms, suppressing the turbulence. "Shhh, shhh . . ."

"But—"

"Let's stop and think for a minute. Who's the boss of Shakespeare Club?"

They look at each other.

"Um . . . you?" Grace offers. *Thanks for the vote of confidence.*

"That's correct. I'm the boss. Now, would I *ever* let anyone else come in here and take over, or be mean to you—or *direct the play*, for cryin' out loud?"

"No?" Carla asks.

"That's right, I wouldn't."

"But Dana said we could have a party!" Carla adds.

Well played, Dana. She's set me up good.

"Dana's chock full of stories, isn't she? Let's start rehearsal."

Marin has arrived with Miles and Jennifer, but others are missing.

"Where is everybody?"

Maybe Dana ate them for lunch. I want to hunt her down, but we're at the final rehearsal, *and* four cast members are AWOL.

At the door, I bump into Stella.

"Hi, Stella!" But her face is ashen.

"Hi." She casually passes me, drops her backpack, and moves far away.

Candace rushes in, gasping for air.

"Candace? What's going on?"

Candace looks at Stella. Stella looks at Candace.

"Girls, what is it?"

Candace blurts out the latest drama.

"Anna said the B-word! She didn't mean to . . . but she was so mad—"

"She said the B-word to Jordan," Stella jumps in. She's attempting to look pious. She's failing.

I ask Candace to give me the details.

"Jordan said stuff to Anna and then Anna used the B-word, but she just did it because she was so frustrated and she didn't mean to, so now Anna is inside the toilet and she's crying . . . bad."

"Get your props and scripts ready to rehearse. I'll be right back."

Once again, I march across the grounds. Stella and Candace tag along, trying to keep up. As we near the bathroom, Jordan joins our group. We look like a grim version of the final parade from *The Music Man*.

"Anna called me the B-word!" Jordan shouts. I pick up the pace, leaving her in the dust.

"And why do you think she did that, Jordan?" I call back.

"I don't know!"

"I think you do!"

"But the B-word is really bad, and she really said it!"

Jordan is adamant, and it bugs me.

"I guess we'll find out, won't we?" I say as I push the bathroom door open.

In *A Midsummer Night's Dream*, Shakespeare spins a tale of mortals going crazy in a forest. Irrational behavior abounds, characters fall in love with those they've never liked, fairies flit and fly, and madness reigns.

It's not unlike the scene in the girls' bathroom.

From the larger wheelchair-accessible stall at the end of the room, I can hear Anna weeping. I knock lightly.

"Anna, it's Ms. Ryane . . . can you let me in?"

And she does, which surprises me. Sometimes, I forget I'm with children. An adult would tell me to bugger off.

I step inside the stall, Candace and Stella on my tail and Jordan not far behind. It's quite spacious, as bathroom stalls go. An opaque window filters bright sunlight from outside. Anna has backed herself into a corner. As reported, she's crying hard. Her cheeks are wet, and her nose is running. She swallows the sobs percolating from her skinny chest. Her pink boa is draped toward the floor in sadness.

"Anna, tell me what happened," I say softly.

She struggles between crying bouts to reveal the story.

"I said the B-word . . . I just did it . . . I couldn't help it . . . but I just got so tired." More tears.

I touch her shoulder. "Anna, it's okay. I know you said a bad word, but I want to know what happened. What made you so angry?"

She warily assesses the other girls. They hang onto her every word.

"I get so tired because . . . they make fun . . . they make fun if I have the answer and they call me teacher's pet . . . and what I wear and if I'm smart . . . they say I'm a nerd . . . and I just get so tired of it. . . . I didn't mean to but . . . then they pulled my backpack and . . . the stuff . . . my stuff came out and the names . . . they don't stop . . . I feel all by myself . . . I'm so . . . so . . . stupid. . . ."

Anna's sobs overtake her.

I'm stunned I'd missed this. All this time, all these weeks, all these months, I thought Anna was fine in her singularity. I thought she was immune. I thought wrong.

I reach for her and notice her backpack on the ground. It's ripped open. Books, papers, and pens are scattered across the tile floor. Stella, Jordan, and Candace stare at Anna. The guilty cats bearing witness to the mouse's tale.

Good God, how did this happen? I'm in a bathroom with the cast of *Mean Girls*.

I moved to New York City in the mid-eighties armed with a solid resume, a steady grip on my craft, and a determination to make a dream come true. I wanted to do Shakespeare in the Park. After that, I wanted a show on Broadway.

I knew actors who had moved to Los Angeles, but not me. I didn't need a television series or a movie career. I wanted the real thing: New York, New York.

In front of the casting department of the Public Theater, I completed what actors call our "party pieces." One classical and one modern monologue. I won't lie; I rocked. The two casting women stared at me from across a table in the cavernous rehearsal hall. They perused my resume. Nothing was said . . . for too long a time, in my opinion.

"Nice skirt," the brunette said, finally breaking the silence.

"Yeah, really nice," the blonde agreed. "Is that suede?'

"Well," the brunette sighed, "you're great . . . terrific. I'll be eager to follow your career. I think you'll do very well in the city."

What about in here, for starters?

"How do you see your career going?" the blonde asked.

"My dream is Shakespeare in the Park," I gushed. "I moved here with that in mind."

"Ahhh," the brunette answered, "and you do have a lot of classical credits. Thing is, right now at the Public, we're looking for actors who haven't done Shakespeare to do Shakespeare in the Park."

Casting 1, Nitwit 0.

As it turns out, this was exactly what happened, and I had no argument with it. They wanted to cast kids off the street. Hip-hop breakdancers and buskers to do Shakespeare, and it made sense freshness-wise. It was just rotten timing for my arrival in New York City.

I took the red 1 Line uptown to check out Broadway, where the leggy Vegas star Susan Anton was doing the serious David Rabe play, *Hurlyburly*. I didn't have the legs; all I had was Shakespeare and a good skirt.

Further uptown, my agent set up a meeting with the casting department at ABC television. A little TV would be all right. New York actors do that all the time. A soap opera in the day and a play at night. Maybe off-Broadway, that's the ticket . . . this could work out fine.

"You're a wonderful actress," the casting director said, "but you'll never work for ABC." She continued to view my resume. "We're a T&A network," she explained, putting my resume down and folding her hands on top of it. "We're a jiggle network, and you . . . don't."

I never did work for ABC.

Casting 2, Flat Chest 0.

For three years, I stuck it out in New York. I worked six days a week teaching aerobics four classes a day. Contrary to what one might think, this does not put one in good shape. This puts one in a hospital—except I couldn't go there without insurance. When I wasn't jumping up and down, I waitressed and held a part-time job at a PR firm.

In New York City, I got really tired.

And then off-off, way-off-Broadway there was a play and others, even further away: New Mexico, San Diego, Alabama.

And after that, I bought a ticket to Los Angeles. It was time to reset my goals. Get a television series and *then* let Broadway beg for me. And when they called, maybe I'd have time to fit in a little Shakespeare in the Park for laughs.

I wipe away Anna's tears with a tissue.

"You're not alone. It's not a crime to be smart and have the answers. Someone here thinks you're special and perfect just as you are. Someone here thinks you're going to go the distance and have a fantastic life because you're not like everyone else."

"You?" She looks up with a slurp.

"Yes, Anna, me. Don't give in. Be the person you want to be, always. You were frustrated, and you used that word. I forgive you, and you must forgive yourself."

Anna blows her nose, gathers her stuff, and picks up her backpack. I face the posse.

"You girls did something nasty here, and you know it. Jordan, Anna feels terrible for calling you a name, but you have to take responsibility for your part in this. Anna will say she's sorry, and you will as well. Anna?"

"Sorry . . . sorry for calling you the B-word," Anna says.

I cock my head at Jordan. She stares back. I lift my eyebrows.

"No! No, I'm not saying sorry because *she* said the B-word!"

"Jordan, I can't tell you how disappointed I am. And I'm sick of hearing this garbage about the B-word. Anna apologized, and you must as well. Do you remember the mottos of the Shakespeare Club?"

Jordan shakes her head, refusing to say anything.

"You guys are pissing me off."

"Ms. Ryane—"

"Zip it, Candace. Stella, tell me about the backpack."

"I just saw it lying down . . . I didn't know it was Anna's—"

"I don't believe you. If you want to impress me, you'll also apologize to Anna. If you don't, I'll be as disappointed with you as I am with Jordan and her lame-brain decision."

Stella won't go out on a limb because Jordan won't. Candace won't because no one else will. They'd all participated in taunting Anna. They'd circled and tore apart her backpack. I feel sick thinking about it. It was malicious, sadistic, bullying behavior. They'd batted Anna and watched her squirm and spin. It's a cruel picture in my head.

I take Anna's hand and make tracks.

"Let's go girls, we have rehearsal." I'm cold and efficient.

"Well, I'm *not* going to say—"

"Quiet, Jordan," I cut her off. "The only words from your mouth for the rest of the day better be Shakespeare's. Same goes for you, Stella and Candace."

We return to Room 15, and everybody takes their seats.

On the board: FINAL REHEARSAL.

All ten actors sit with scripts in laps and props under chairs. It's quiet as I consider how close we are to the end of our journey.

"Before we start our warm-up," I say, "I have one last prop to hand out."

At home, in our garage, I'd cut out a square of cardboard and painted it a rusty red. With black paint, I drew rectangles in the shape of bricks. Over all of this, in purples, pinks, greens, blues, and yellows, I painted swirls of vines and flowers with a dragonfly and a butterfly buzzing around.

I'd made a wall.

With ceremony, I hang this wall over Carla's neck. It rests on her tummy, held up by a string of green wool.

Carla looks down at her "costume" and blushes.

"Thank you, Ms. Ryane. I love my wall."

The bitterness of Anna's scenario gives way to our last rehearsal and the tenderness of a little girl enthralled by a cardboard wall.

"Now, before we start our run-through, we need to talk about how we behave in front of an audience. Next Thursday, you'll arrive in the auditorium as soon as school has finished, and we'll do our warm-up. When we're ready, we'll let the audience in and wait in our chairs while they get seated."

"Ms. Ryane, are kids coming?" Jennifer asks.

"I don't know who's coming, but I do know you'll be ready for anything and anyone."

Jennifer chews on the prospect of kids coming.

"Here's what we *don't* do." I pace in front of them. "We don't wave at people we know, or jump up to get someone's attention, or point out when our part is coming up . . . do you understand what I mean? We don't want to be cheesy."

Cheesy is a good kid word. They love it and repeat it, laughing and shouting. "Cheesy!"

"Okay," I call out. "I suggest right now we pretend it's show day. Let's get *cheesy* out of our systems. On the count of three, I'll pretend to be the audience and you be super cheesy to get my attention."

On three, Miles leaps out of his seat and throws his arm around to get my attention. Carla does her yell, and Stella makes her lion roar. They hop and dance and laugh. Regina twirls, and Jordan and Candace shout, "Me! Me! Look at me!" Marin and Jennifer scream over each other, "Hey, here I am!" and "Over here, I'm the best!"

Even Anna gets into it, transforming into a happier girl.

With this energy, we dive into a run-through and, true to theatrical tradition . . . it's lousy.

But tradition also holds that a bad dress rehearsal portends a good opening. This thought crosses my mind as I watch the mess in front of me. *Good lord, what have I wrought?* They're scattered and forget to read the chorus. Lines are dropped, entrances and exits missed, and Miles bumbles over the word *love* as if he's just visited the cootie factory.

The rehearsal is a full-fledged disaster, and, worst of all, they're oblivious. They think it's just dandy. They're actually having fun, which burns me up. They giggle and cavort. They shove each other onto center stage. The fairies speed around Titania, screeching the lullaby. Lysander and Demetrius come perilously close to impaling one another with their plastic swords. Helena and Hermia hurl insults at each other while facing upstage, as if the audience will be interested in watching the backs of their heads.

All those weeks, all those hours, and all those private sessions in the library are a distant memory. I rub my head to erase the ache crawling up my neck.

It's so damn tragic because we came so close but now are so far, far away from anything even resembling a "staged reading" of an adaptation of William Shakespeare's *A Midsummer Night's Dream*.

Later, Room 15 is quiet and empty. The mayhem has ended, the props lie still, and the backpacks have been lugged out the door. Exhausted, I drag the chairs back into place and untangle the purple and pink ribbons of the fairy wreaths. Oberon's gold crown is dented, and Bottom's donkey head has bent ears. Puck's purple flower has been tossed under a chair, and Peter Quince's cast list is sadly crumpled.

I sigh, grateful for the silence, but not for much else.

I'd made a vow, and it was time to implement it. This belongs to them now, to do with as they wish. *How will they learn anything if I don't let them fail?*

I zip up my script binder and notice a card tucked under my notes. It's an invitation to a concert. "Strings by the Sea" is performing next week. Another violinist had continued the after-school music program Orlantha Ambrose had started. Apparently, someone would like me to attend.

Both Grace and Marin play violin in the program. I flag down Grace on the grounds and ask her about the concert.

"I'm not in the concert, but Marin is."

Could I possibly miss Marin's violin performance after she so shyly tipped me off? I could not.

In the auditorium, parents, grandparents, and a few teachers gather. Toddlers speed on chubby legs up and down the aisles. Marin's grandmother, Helen, provides refreshments in the courtyard, a buffet of tiny quiches, chips, drinks, and cookies.

I sit in the back. The curtains creak open to reveal eight tall girls dressed in black skirts and white blouses, one tall boy in black trousers and a white shirt, and, at the stage's edge, a small, thin girl in a black skirt, a ruffled blouse, and brilliant white sandals on her feet.

I have never seen Marin in a dress. Her hair is pulled into a ponytail, and her violin is tucked under her chin as she focuses on the conductor.

As I watch Marin play, I think about how I'd almost kicked her out of the Shakespeare Club, about how disruptive she used to be. This girl drawing a bow over strings is the same child who threw pillows, kicked boys, and elbowed anyone who drifted into her space. I think about how I'd struggled to earn Marin's trust. She'd challenged me, tested me, and made me jump through her hoops. She wasn't wrong to do that. I was inconvenienced, but it was necessary for our relationship. Marin had her way, and I had to learn it.

In the auditorium, a serious child is in command of both her violin and the most difficult instrument to master, her own heart. The image of Marin and her violin will move me always as it did that day.

CHILDREN'S WRITES

Dear Jirnal,
What I learned about Shakespeare? I learned that he had 3 chledren and his fist jode was to be a water doy. On stage he wasll so was a riter. he also was a play riter.

LESSON PLAN

Be a leader. Quit trying to fix.

On a recent summer day, I strolled through Central Park and the Upper West Side. I had a hankering to explore my old neighborhood. The sun was warm, and the sky was as blue and cloudless as a theatrical cyclorama. The city had changed since my days of struggle. It was difficult to find a Greek coffee shop for thick French toast. Chain stores and fancy restaurants had replaced many mom-and-pop businesses.

Even so, the park was stunning. New Yorkers picnicked, read newspapers, batted baseballs, and chatted while their tiny ones chased pigeons. I exited the park and cut across to the Fairway market, where I savored the sights and aromas of my past. Pungent cheeses and smoked meats. Piles of oranges, pears, and plums, sweet and ripe. Scarlet raspberries stacked next to fat blueberries. The Fairway had been my grocery of choice. As I wandered the aisles, jostling my way through the crowds, I comforted my young, desperate, and sad self.

"Now aren't you glad you lived?" I asked her.

"Yeah," she whispered back.

My resume grew in Los Angeles. I acted in television shows and theatre until a day when my checking account contained a total of seven dollars. I had no auditions lined up. Waitress, aerobics teacher, receptionist, telemarketer, casting assistant, bookseller, craft service assistant, theatrical manager, dialogue coach, acting coach, voice coach.

Actor.

I don't regret one second.

The map of my life opens as crisp and clean as a 100% pure white cotton sheet.

The map tells a journey of two countries—countries where oceans hold the land tight on either side—countries where Arctic mass and burning desert press in from top to bottom.

The map of my life marks the route of twenty-four homes, thirteen jobs, seven cars, five cities, four cats, three husbands, and one woman.

The map of my life traces footprints, skid marks, potholes, and whiteouts—

But still—

The map of my life opens as crisp and clean as a 100% pure white cotton sheet.

Life 10, Casting 0.

CHAPTER XIX

"I ALWAYS KNEW I WANTED TO BE AN ACTOR, MY WHOLE LIFE!"

We few, we happy few, we band of brothers;
For he to-day that sheds his blood with me
Shall be my brother . . . .

Henry V Act IV, Scene III

Bang! Bang! BANG!

Ten children are facing me from their chairs in the auditorium, so it can't be any one of them up to their old tricks at the locked door. I ignore it.

We have exactly half an hour to warm up and prepare for an audience. The music stand is in place for Marin, the kids are seated in a half-circle in front of the stage and—

BANG! BANG! BANG!

For God's sake.

"Just a second . . . let me see what this is about," I say.

I'd locked the doors so we could have some privacy, but someone is demanding entrance. I stride to the door with a tight jaw and profanity filling my head. I yank it open, and Mr. Davis pushes past me.

"I have to use the bathroom!" he explains, moving quickly.

The bathroom? Is this the only bathroom in the entire school?

"Wow, Mr. Davis really has to pee," Marin says.

"Okay, let's get to it," I bubble to block out the interruption.

"Ms, Ryane, I can't do this," Jennifer calls out. "Kids are coming, I just know it!"

"I'm so nervous!" Stella screams.

"We can't, Ms. Ryane, it's too scary," Regina says.

"You know what? I'd be scared if you weren't scared. Being scared means you care about telling this story. You're supposed to be nervous, it's natural . . . it's a good sign. All actors, even big fat movie stars, get nervous."

"I'm not scared," Anna says.

Candace looks doubtful, and I shoot her a smile. She's wearing her blue BABY DOLL satin jacket, no longer shiny but dull with wear. Jordan wears her hoodie, no longer black but faded and sooty. Today, despite their garb, the twins will rise above their struggles to play seven parts between them. Today, they'll become actors.

"We should get cheesy out of our systems!" Carla screams.

"Yes, we should get cheesy out of our systems," I agree, and so they do. They shriek and scream in an exuberant outpour.

I paw the air to instill peace. They settle, with eyes on me.

"It's the responsibility of the actors to check that their props are in order."

They look under their chairs and softly touch crowns and fairy wreaths. I slide Miles's sword into his belt loop, and he runs his fingers over the gold plastic. Grace has her purple flower, Regina holds her lantern, and Carla caresses her wall.

I cruise around the train of chairs and pause at each actor to inject a final piece of encouragement.

"Miles, you're the bravest boy in school." He tilts up, surprised. "It hasn't been easy to be the only boy in Shakespeare Club, but you found the courage. I'm proud of you."

He shrugs, a little embarrassed.

"Carla, you wear the wall well. You've learned to use your voice, and that's fantastic."

"Regina, I want to praise your moon to the moon because it puts me over the moon."

"Anna, your Titania is as beautiful as you are. Congratulations on learning all your lines."

"Candace, you've come such a long way. You deserve to have the time of your life, and you will."

"Jordan, you came back to us when you didn't think you could. I'm happy to know you."

Jordan reddens, looks to her lap and beams.

"Stella, your decision to give up whining is the biggest change I've seen anyone make. Have a good show, Hermia."

"Jennifer, use your big voice, and remember I'll be missing you next year when you're in Mexico."

"Grace, you were the first to know your lines. I like to think of you going to sleep next to your little Globe Theatre. 'What fools these mortals be,' Grace. Sing it out."

I reach Marin at her music stand. Her face is clear and sober. I touch her shoulder. "Marin, I've learned from you that first impressions aren't always right."

She gives me a quizzical look.

"I watched you play violin last week."

Her look blooms into a wide smile.

"As you played, you showed a discipline I didn't know you had when we met. And you brought that to *A Midsummer Night's Dream*. Remember when I said you were a leader? You are."

Marin looks ready to burst.

We deep breathe. We let bumblebees buzz around in our mouths. We do Child's Pose and run through the chorus parts of the play.

"Ready?" I whisper.

They look at each other, squirm, and give me serious nods.

"I'll be in the front row. If you need a line, I'll be right here."

I open the auditorium doors. Family members and a few teachers file down the aisles and take seats. Much to Jennifer's chagrin, children arrive—but not too many. The actors silently stare at their audience.

The auditorium is barely half full, and there are some important missing persons.

"Ms. Ryane, can we please wait a little? My mom's not here." Regina is desperate.

"Of course."

The principal arrives, and I'm moved as she shakes each child's hand, congratulating them for being members of the Shakespeare Club. Miles's face registers utter astonishment as she takes his hand. He might as well be meeting Queen Elizabeth.

And then we wait. The clock ticks and tocks for an agonizing and heartrending length of time.

I ask the principal if late arrivals are normal.

"Yes," she confirms, "it's very common. Let's give it a little longer."

The kids are worried.

"My mom's not here!"

"My dad's not here!"

"Please, Ms. Ryane, just wait, please."

So we do. We wait forty minutes as parents and relatives dribble in.

Restless, I scoot up and down the aisle as ten extremely patient actors gaze out front. Regina's mom ambles up the walk, chatting to a friend as if she were entering a supermarket to pick up some milk.

I want to scream at her. Instead, I smile and say, "We're about to begin. . . ."

She glances at me like I'm a checkout girl. I bite my tongue.

By 3:45, I decide we have to start. The principal introduces me, and I join her in front of the children. I'm as nervous as they are. *Are we making history?*

The audience, now settled, gives their full attention. Parents wave and call out, but not one actor reciprocates. Cheesy has left the building.

"These children look like regular students of Arden Street Elementary, but I assure you they are not. They are Shakespearean actors, here to perform William Shakespeare's *A Midsummer Night's Dream.*"

I turn to the cast and give them a wink before I take my seat in the front row. Pale faces look back at me.

Fly, little birds.

Decent directors know that you prepare actors, get them to the brink, and gently push them onstage. Good parents know this also holds true for raising children. Remarkable directors, teachers, and parents suffer the hard truth: to sit on your hands and keep your mouth shut is near impossible. But somehow that afternoon, I do.

Marin takes a courageous look at her audience. I inhale with her, lean forward, and open my mouth as she opens hers.

> NARRATOR
> *Our play is set in Athens, where Duke Theseus will marry
> Hippolyta. But first, the Duke must have a meeting with Egeus.*

Her voice is low, but it grows in strength as she continues. Marin is learning on the spot that she is worth hearing. She has finally abandoned her campaign for attention, instead finding it in the words of William Shakespeare. I relax.

"Mel, you're a good actor, but you don't allow us to be a part of it. You must share. You must let the audience in. That's what you're here for," said the director.

I remember my shock upon learning that being an honest actor wasn't enough. That my imagination was the starting point, not the finish line.

As Theseus and Egeus berate Hermia and Lysander, the actors form their familiar huddle. They step together closer and closer, and my stomach clenches as they make a tiny circle and shut the audience out. *Share, share . . . open, open . . .*

As if they can hear me, they start to cheat their bodies downstage. I exhale.

The moms, dads, and teachers are alert and listening. The beautiful marriage of audience and actor is taking place. I'm pleased as the kids recite the chorus in one voice. That simply has never happened before—not in one single rehearsal.

Stella sings out, "So will I grow, so live, so die, my lord." Like a professional ham, she bathes in shouts of spectator approval.

Miles matches her line for line as the lovers plan their exit to the forest. As he lifts his sword to Demetrius's, he's steady and disciplined. Miles and Lysander have made peace. Jennifer pushes hard to use her outside voice. She succeeds. Despite her shyness, she's acting.

The six jolly men leap to center stage—but they're joined by a seventh, not-so-jolly man. An unexpected player has shuffled into the auditorium: a wraith-like janitor with a wrinkled face is wheeling a creaking garbage can across our stage. A hanging broom clangs on the side of the can. Oblivious to our production, he steers his canister upstage and starts sweeping the floor. He has a job to do, and he's doing it.

I'm aghast and can hardly stay seated. The principal and vice-principal are smothering fits of giggles. I chew my tongue to calm my twitching. Amazingly, neither the actors nor the audience are thrown by this intrusion as the bumbling fellow wanders off . . . *creak, squeak, clang* . . . to tidy up elsewhere.

Candace tears up the stage with her Nick Bottom. In her donkey mask, she regales Titania.

"Hee haw, hee haw!"

Arms spread, she holds the crowd in the palm of her ten-year-old hand.

When Jordan, as Peter Quince, berates Bottom, something sparks between the sisters and sends them into gut-splitting laughter. It's free, crazy, and purely joyful. Their merriment is contagious; the audience joins in on the fun. Jordan and Candace are convulsing in pee-your-pants hysteria. Gone are the tears, the doubts, the battles. They're having a ball, and I'm thrilled.

As Titania, queen of the fairies, Anna is wearing an elegant ensemble consisting of a chocolate-brown dress, a cream lace vest, and, of course, her matching pink boa. As she sheds the skin of schoolyard victim, she transforms into a leading lady.

Titania's fairies join hands and circle her, singing. We've rehearsed this bit a lot. It's intended as a gentle moment as Titania is guided into slumber. Today, however, adrenaline amplifies the lullaby into a screaming mania. Carla's wreath flies off her head as she loses her grip on Jordan's hand. The fairies spin out of control, barely staying upright. They gain momentum around poor Anna, lying somewhat vulnerable in the middle.

At last the reveling fairies settle down and grab their seats, sweaty and panting. Anna remains unscathed.

Crowns and swords are spirited hand to hand, shared by many actors playing many parts. *Swoosh* slides a plastic blade under three chairs to land at the foot of the next actor who needs it.

With a wreath of flowers on her head and a purple flower in her hand, Grace recites, "What fools these mortals be" and flashes me a grin. I give her a big thumbs-up.

I'll be right here if you need me. That never happened. They never needed me. They ran with it. When problems arose, they solved them on their own. They depended on each other and helped each other. Nudged each other to make entrances, grab props, kneel, and bow. Like real actors in a real show.

I'm hard-pressed to pick a favorite moment from our performance, but if I had to, I'd choose Carla belting out her lines as the wall. A ripple of excitement radiated from the audience as she took center stage wearing her outfit. Her family, hands held in prayer, hung onto her every word.

As she took her seat, we all cheered for her.

Marin is standing as the play comes to a close. She grins at her cast mates. Marin knows it's all about to end as she begins the final chorus. The fifth-graders,

Anna, Candace, and Jordan, know this is farewell. They will be off to another school next fall, and their adventure with the Shakespeare Club will be complete.

The actors speak, as one, with Marin.

CHORUS
If we shadows have offended,
Think but this, and all will be mended:
That you have but slumb'red here,
While these visions did appear.
Give me your hands, if we be friends,
And Puck shall restore amends.

The audience explodes into cheers and applause. The actors rise, startled. They look like a juvenile police lineup. I give them a signal, and they bow. Once, twice, three times . . . and then they all burst out laughing.

The adored father of Candace and Jordan has limped in on a cane during the curtain call, the end of the performance. Their mother had arrived on time, but the girls ignored her. Now they run to their dad, hugging him and hopping up and down and squealing.

The principal puts her hand on my shoulder.

"Mel, I knew this would be good, but I didn't expect it to be great. Believe me, I know these kids. And they were fantastic today."

Stella runs up and wraps her arms around me, giggling.

"I always knew I wanted to be an actor, my whole life!"

"And, Stella, that's what happened." I touch her forehead. "You waited eight long years to act, and today, you did."

What happened this day is miraculous, as is the case when art surpasses expectation.

During our battles, I never thought the kids would deliver anything beyond an ordinary recitation of the play. I was wrong. These ten kids held hands and climbed a golden mountain . . . together. Like the children spirited away in my revision of the Pied Piper legend, they went to a better place.

When that flyer, asking for help, appeared on our porch, the smartest thing I did was to go through the front door and find the courage to go through a bigger door. The second smartest thing was not quitting.

I've spent many thrilling nights onstage during my acting career. There were days when I was as happy as Stella because I acted, angels flew close, and it worked. There were also nights when I lay on my bedroom floor, weeping and begging those angels to explain why I'd been given such a useless gift.

What the hell am I supposed to do off the stage, when the well is dry? What is my talent for?

This. This day.

CHILDREN'S WRITES

How did I feel performing the play in front of people. I felt very scared. I felt nervous. I thought I was going to faint. When people stared clapping I was very shy. When the play finished I was crazy! It was very fun.

LESSON PLAN

They will surprise you. You will never be bored.

During my last year of high school, a drama teacher suggested I enter a youth Shakespeare competition. It would take place downtown and be adjudicated by an older professional theatre actor. I chose Juliet's potion speech and rehearsed for months with the help of my teacher. To say I was influenced by Olivia Hussey in Zeffirelli's production would be an understatement. To say I'd been waiting to play Juliet from the day I discovered her in a dusty cabin couldn't be more accurate.

My mother and I chose white fabric spun from linen and cotton. She would sew me a full-length nightgown gathered at the neckline, with long sleeves cuffed in puckered frills. With my dark hair parted in the center, I was certain Zeffirelli himself would approve.

The night before the competition, I did something to upset my mother/costume designer. I don't know what because she wouldn't tell me. Worse, she refused to go near the sewing machine to finish my outfit.

"What? What did I do?" I begged.

"If you don't know, it's pointless."

In the basement, the Singer sat quiet and still, and beyond my abilities. I held up pieces of fabric. An arm, a front section, another arm . . . and I wept. My Juliet was in scraps, and I didn't know how to put her together.

"Mom, please . . . I'm sorry."

Night fell. I didn't sleep for a long time. I tossed, turned, and fumed . . . exactly like Juliet trying to swallow her elixir.

Upon waking, I found the costume, ready and waiting. I'd been terrorized and now it was over.

"Thanks, Mom."

I took to the stage with a tiny bottle held high and Juliet's night horrors racing through me. The nightgown's folds draped to the floor around my bare feet, and I knew I had 'em.

"In second place . . . I think we can agree this was a real Juliet. Congratulations."

I was awarded a score of 97% and given a certificate with my name on it.

Neither my mother nor I could have predicted Juliet's nightgown would be her last costume for me. Neither of us could have guessed that within months, I'd be on my first professional stage.

I always knew I wanted to be an actor, my whole life!

William and I have a tradition. Well, I came up with it, and he indulges me. On our anniversary, we list our favorite moments from the past year. At our favorite French bistro, we share a bottle of wine, slurp mussels, and swap memories.

William chooses a warm summer evening we had spent at a Dodgers game. I pick the long walk through rainy San Francisco. But he surprises me with his first choice.

"The day the Shakespeare Club did *A Midsummer Night's Dream*."

"You weren't even there. You were working."

"But I saw it in your face that night. I saw it in your eyes, every minute of it. That's my favorite moment."

CHAPTER XX

AND SO . . .

With one "We thank you" many thousands moe
That go before it.

The Winter's Tale Act I, Scene II

I don't know what she's thinking . . . why she wants to do this, go back with him. He's a bad guy, Ms. Ryane. He broke out of jail or something . . . I don't know what she's thinking . . ."

Candace and I sit across from each other at a picnic table as I videotape her. I'd asked each of the ten kids to do an on-camera interview with me about their experiences in the Shakespeare Club.

I started with a question to Candace: "What are your plans for the summer?"

"Not much. Me and Jordan are moving."

"Where are you going?"

"Lancaster or Palmdale or something . . . with my mom. First, we have to go to a motel till school finishes and then up there, somewhere."

"Up there" is the high desert. A hot, windy landscape quite unlike the breezy coast where the girls live with their dad. As she speaks, Candace pushes aside tendrils of hair and rests her forehead on a hand. She looks exhausted. She wears the bewildered look of a parent at wits' end raising a volatile child. She shakes her head and repeats, "I just don't know what she's thinking."

I shut the camera off. This is not where I'd intended the interview to go. What is this mother thinking? She's uprooting her daughters to live in the desert with an ex-con? "Candace, this is for you."

I hand her a paperback copy of *A Midsummer Night's Dream*.

"Thanks, Ms. Ryane."

"Look inside."

She opens the cover to my note saying how proud I am of her performance as Nick Bottom. How I know that wherever life takes her, she'll always do well. Below my signature, I've written my email address and phone number.

I secretly hope if she ever needs help, she'll let me know.

"Candace, you love to write. I hope you'll always keep a journal. Write down your dreams, your feelings, and your thoughts because they're important. They're yours, and no one can take them away from you."

Our final Shakespeare Club meeting is back in the library, where we first met. The kids gather on the storytime risers. I look at them. The library, of course, is exactly the same. We are not.

We gaze at each other. Shy smiles break out as I pan over the kids.

"Next year, there will be some changes in the Shakespeare Club. For starters, everyone will have to audition to get in."

"I want to do Shakespeare Club again, Ms. Ryane, and what play will we be doing, anyway?" Stella asks.

"I haven't decided yet."

"Grace and me are going to audition," Carla says.

"Me too," Regina adds.

"You learned this year that a play requires hard work. Next year, we'll have to work a little harder."

"No, Ms. Ryane," Marin calls out from the back row, "a *lot* harder."

"You got it. A *lot* harder."

I give them twenty minutes to make final entries in their journals. Candace writes like a torch has been lit under her. Regina sidles next to me and looks up with a smile.

"I'm glad you stuck with us, aren't you?" I ask her.

"Yes."

"What did you like most about Shakespeare Club?"

"The old stuff . . . kings and queens and stuff."

I'd called her wrong. Regina's interest wasn't in acting but in history. The "old stuff."

Miles is crazy excited. He hops up and down and thrusts a gift bag into my hands. I open it up to find a set of earrings.

"Miles, how very thoughtful. Thank you."

"And . . . and . . . also . . . my mom has stuff. . . ." Miles points toward tables outside where some mothers have arranged cupcakes and juice boxes.

Before our final party, I ask them to gather one last time in a circle.

"I was honored to work with each of you this year in the Shakespeare Club. Jennifer's moving to Mexico, and we say goodbye to her and wish her all the best on her journey. Jordan, Candace, and Anna are off to middle school. We'll miss you."

They listen as I stumble through my speech. I could have used some rehearsal myself because I find myself trembling.

"Mostly, I want to say thank you. Thank you for letting me do this with you. I had the best time."

And the irony hits me. *There's the gratitude.* It makes me blush. The teacher has been taught.

"Can we have our party now?" Anna asks.

"Of course! Party down."

I open the door and hustle them outside.

I take a minute to gather up journals and pens, and I stuff everything back into the Shakespeare Club box. Captain Underpants gives me an A-okay. I give him a thumbs-up.

In the sunny courtyard, my head rattles with ideas for next fall. I'll get the school's booster club to pay for Shakespeare Club T-shirts . . . I'll show them Zeffirelli's film of *Romeo and Juliet* . . . we'll do *two* performances . . . I'll have a picnic dinner in between shows . . . I'll recruit more boys . . . we'll do new yoga poses . . . I'll stage the swordfights . . . I'll show them the Simpsons doing *Hamlet.* . . .

The kids are gobbling chocolate cupcakes and red-hot Cheetos, and I ask them what they want to be when they grow up. Miles is too shy to tell me, but his cousin, Jennifer, isn't.

She blurts it out for him. "Miles wants to be in the CIA."

"The CIA, Miles?"

He nods.

"You'll make a good spy. You've got the whole hiding thing down."

"Hey, Ms. Ryane!" from across the playground.

"Hey, Daniel!" I wave. "Have a swell summer."

"Okay!" he shouts, and takes off.

The next day is the school's Heritage Day celebration. Each class performs a dance or musical number. It's like a Cinco de Mayo celebration. Red, white, and green streamers flutter over the courtyard.

A tiny first-grader stands on tiptoe at the microphone. In a big voice, she announces her class. I grab her teacher's arm.

"What's her name? She'll be perfect for Shakespeare Club."

Two years from now, she'll be in third grade and eligible for the club and . . .

Two years later, this child played Juliet. Brilliantly.

Carnival games are set up on the grounds. Children buy cotton candy and burritos. Volunteers have labored to stuff confetti into emptied-out eggshells, which kids gleefully crack on top of each other's heads. Parents gather to chat while their offspring tear around the yard, screaming and laughing.

I wander among them, looking for Charley, my reading buddy.

"Hi, Charley!" I say when I spot him.

He beams at me with an eggshell in his hand.

"Having fun?" I ask.

Charley nods, and I kneel beside him.

"I'll see you in the fall, okay?"

"Are you going to read with me again?"

"Yes, I am. We have lots more books to read."

"And also in third grade and after that?"

"Yes, Charley. I'm going to read with you until you finish fifth grade and leave Arden Street. Does that sound like a good plan?"

He nods and runs off to crack a friend on the head.

As I leave the party, I see Marin, alone.

"Hey, you!" I say. "Have a terrific summer."

Marin suddenly grabs me around the waist and buries her face in my stomach. I kiss the top of her head. This is unexpected from a girl known to be a reluctant hugger.

"I'll see you next year, right?"

"Right." She looks up.

We separate, and from across the field, another small figure barrels toward me.

"Hey, Miles!"

He hugs me, too.

"Did people say nice things after your performance?"

"Yeah."

"That felt pretty good, I bet."

"Yeah."

"Miles, I'll see you next year."

"Okay!" He tears off.

As I drive away, I look in the mirror and see a schoolyard filled with running children, colorful streamers, and flying bits of pastel paper. It's the picture of fun. It's a celebration. It's what they'll remember.

It looks Elizabethan.

CHILDREN'S WRITES

How did I feel performing the play of Midsummer Nights Dream? When I first enterd Shakespeare I thought it was going to be boring but it was very fun. I love Shakespeare.

LESSON PLAN

Let them go. There will be more right behind them.

"Do you miss acting?" This is a question I'm sometimes asked.

And I answer, "I never miss the *career* of an actor, but every once in a while, I'll see an inspired performance or hear great writing . . . and yeah, I do, a little."

I attended a play a couple of years ago where a young actress ran onstage in moonlight. She wore a long white gown, her dark hair fell to her shoulders, and her cheeks shone pink. I saw myself. I miss *her*. I miss my ingénue.

In her, I saw the belief, the commitment, and the trust of being onstage with the words, actions, and the almighty need to tell a story. An actor knows what tear ducts are for. An actor earns laugh lines like no one else. An actor's lungs are huge.

For a long time, I thought if I wasn't in a show, I wasn't an interesting person. If I wasn't acting, I wasn't truly alive.

I recently read some of my writing to an audience of about fifty people. William came to see me, and I realized, as I stood at the podium, that he'd never seen me perform. He'd never seen me in front of an audience. It went well. He was proud. And I knew it didn't matter.

With that, I let my ingénue go.

ENCORE

If it be true that good wine needs no bush,
'tis true that a good play needs no epilogue.
Yet to good wine they do use good bushes;
and good plays prove the better by the help of good epilogues.

As You Like It Epilogue

Geoffrey, you're playing Horatio."

Geoffrey nods, solemn.

"It's a great part. You watch your best friend, Hamlet, go through all his troubles, but you can't save him, and you're the only major character in the play that isn't killed."

"Yes," Geoffrey says.

"Then you have one of the most beautiful lines that Shakespeare has ever written. As Hamlet is dying in your arms, you say, ' . . . and flights of angels sing thee to thy rest.'"

Geoffrey's dark hair is shaved short. He has clear brown eyes and a roly-poly body. His skin is the color of milky coffee, and freckles are scattered across his nose and cheeks. He listens to me, very serious. I lean in close to him.

"I'm here to help you play this part. You can ask me anything."

He looks down at his script as we sit across from each other in an otherwise empty classroom. He toys with the corner of a page for a while, then meets my eyes.

"Ms. Ryane, when I say that line, I feel like I might almost start crying myself."

He says this with a sense of discovery. As if it might be a bad thing.

Geoffrey is eight. He wears a chocolate-brown leather bomber jacket with a fake fur collar. He rarely takes it off. It can be eighty-five degrees, but that jacket stays on. It's covered in military decals. Tiny crossed rifles, naval ships, and airplanes in flight. Red, blue, and yellow medals decorate Geoffrey's precious bomber jacket.

"My dad's a Navy SEAL," he tells me.

"That's impressive."

"But he's not in the war. He's thirty-five, and that's too young to die."

"It is."

I wonder how that conversation took place. Did Geoffrey worry about his dad leaving for duty? Did his dad miss being "over there"?

"I'm going into cadets next year," he boasts.

"Really . . . so soon?" I try to keep the dismay out of my voice.

"Sure, I can start next year."

"The military is tough," I say. "If those guys got in my face and started shouting, I'd probably burst into tears."

"Yeah, but my dad practices with me. When those guys get in my face and yell, I won't burst into tears . . . I'll be strong. That's discipline."

I look down at my script of *Hamlet*. This is year two of the Shakespeare Club, and Geoffrey is one of eighteen kids who have been selected.

"Geoffrey, I know you'd like to join the military when you grow up, but there's a good chance you could be an actor."

A smile spreads across his face.

"When your family comes to see the play, tell them to bring a mittful of Kleenex 'cause there's going to be some crying going on."

"Yeah," he whispers.

I had to miss a week of Shakespeare Club for jury duty. I joined my fellow citizens in a wood-paneled courthouse downtown. In my eye line were two very young African-American men, small of stature and dressed in shirts and pants that someone had taken the time to iron. They sat side by side with their defense attorneys, a tall, elegant black man in a gray striped suit and a large, jittery Latino man in a rumpled blue suit.

The charges included armed robbery, attempted murder, and two counts of murder, one with special circumstances. Pre-meditated. The judge told us these were gang-related and committed for the purpose of advancing gang stature.

We were warned that, if selected, we'd be viewing photos of the deceased lying on the coroner's table. The victims were a Latino brother and sister, one sixteen years old and the other seventeen. They were shot while sitting in a car.

Soon, two families would gather in this courtroom, a room where the very walls seemed to drip with tragedy. Life is not a movie. There was no rehearsal for this and I had trouble breathing as I listened to the judge.

I stumbled outside during the lunch break. I couldn't see because my eyes were blurry with tears. *Please, God, get me out of this*, I prayed.

"Juror number six," the prosecutor addressed me, and I bolted straight.

She was fine-boned and wore a navy pantsuit with a white blouse. Her hair was streaked blonde on blonde, and though I imagined her to be about thirty-eight, she looked older. Her skin pale, she looked entirely fatigued, as if she hadn't taken a breath of fresh air in a long time.

"Lawyers are cautioned not to choose panelists from the entertainment field," she addressed me. "We're told you like the drama of defendants being set free, and you tend to be liberals."

"Well, I would be wary of lumping all showbiz professionals together. It's a world that attracts many kinds of personalities. Myself, when I coach actors, I'm seeking truth, and I suspect that's what we're here to do," I say.

After two days, I was kicked out by the defense. I was inclined to send them a thank-you note.

Back in the Shakespeare Club, I attempt to erase the image of those young men in their crisp shirts. This is Los Angeles, Hollywood, Tinseltown, with boulevards of broken dreams and red carpets to heaven. On days when the newspaper is too harsh to read, I race to Arden Street Elementary and check a kid out of a classroom.

"Let's work on your script."

A nine-year-old Hamlet laments, "Oh, what a rogue and peasant slave am I."

The reading is sweet, tender, and thrilling.

"Miles, how do you feel when you do this speech?"

"Good."

There's a new strength in Miles' voice. I take his hand.

"Miles, keep doing the work, and I promise, when you do this in front of an audience, you're going to have the best time of your whole life. It's going to blow your mind."

Miles beams. Miles already knows.

"I think I should wear my black shoes when we do it."

"Good idea," I say.

"And my uncle . . . he's a carpenter . . . if I ask him, he'll probably build us a castle."

"I think we're not going to have a real castle, Miles. We just have to imagine that part."

"I could ask him anyway."

I learned from the principal that when Miles started school at Arden Street, he couldn't speak English.

"Miles, when you fill out your college application, be sure to write that you played Hamlet when you were ten."

Compared to my first year, I'm a seasoned pro. I've learned that when boys are bored, they throw themselves to the floor and roll around. This is pure science. When Miles and Geoffrey aren't in boy mayhem, they behave like the best friends Hamlet and Horatio are. They've worked out a cool handshake for whenever they meet onstage. They knock fists, bump shoulders, and bounce off each other's stomachs. They're giving *Hamlet* street cred.

If you'd asked me ten years ago, five years ago . . . *two* years ago if this would be enough to satisfy my creative hunger, I would have laughed and laughed . . . and then I would have cried. No, this wasn't my dream. I've traveled far, expecting to eat caviar . . . but found myself with grilled cheese.

Yet all is right in this world, on an ordinary day in an ordinary public school. After weeks of wending through the play, we've reached the final scene of *Hamlet* in our first run-through.

"Geoffrey . . . ready? This is your moment."

Queen Gertrude is dead, inexplicably clutching a cell phone. Claudius lays crumpled next to her, trying to keep his eyes closed. Hamlet spasmodically twitches on Horatio's lap.

"Miles, be still. You're supposed to be dead," I beg. "Okay, Geoffrey, go for it."

"Hamlet's on my nuts!"

"No, Geoffrey. 'And flights of angels—'"

"He's on my *nuts!*"

Geoffrey hunches his shoulders to his ears. The boy couldn't find his nuts if he came from a family of squirrels, but he's expertly found center stage. In an instant, he's transformed *Hamlet* from tragedy into high-flying comedy. Eighteen kids in the Shakespeare Club share another group laugh.

When these kids graduate from elementary school, they'll walk two blocks south to middle school and, after that, three more blocks to high school. The same high school where not long ago a fifteen-year-old was shot to death by a seventeen-year-old.

I want to encase them in armor. I want to shake their skinny little shoulders and yell at them, "Be careful! Be strong! Please, come back and see me . . . don't disappear."

Life is not a play . . . but it is a tragic comedy. William Shakespeare knew that. His words and stories make for flimsy armor, but maybe, when they need to, these children will remember that they were great. That they surpassed expectations.

The trial took five weeks, and the defendants were found guilty. They were nineteen when the crimes were committed. Each received a sentence of life without parole.

"Ms. Ryane?"

"Geoffrey."

"Will we have to wear tights?"

"I will never make you wear tights. See you next week."

I learned, years later, that Geoffrey had worn his army jacket, even on hot southern Californian days, to cover up bruises.

Midway through the second year, there's a knock on the door during one of our meetings. I open it to three tall girls.

"Hi, Ms. Ryane! Can we come in?"

Anna, Candace, and Jordan. My relief at seeing them is huge. Candace and Jordan look like scoops of sherbet in aqua and pink blouses with their brown, shiny hair pulled into ponytails and their arms opened wide for hugs.

"What happened? I thought you moved."

"Nope," answers Candace. "We said, 'No, we want to stay here. We're not going.'"

Power. They have found it and used it.

"Anna, how are you?"

"I miss Shakespeare Club! We don't have it in middle school, but a play came, *A Comedy of Errors*, and we saw it. It was Shakespeare."

Love. She has found it in the language.

On the day I hand out props for *Hamlet*, a crown falls apart in the hands of the nine-year-old boy playing the ghost. His face scrunches up, and tears streams down his cheeks. He loves his crown, cheap as it was, and thinks he's broken it. I'm across the room engaged in some other problem and can't get to him immediately.

Marin gently takes the crown from Jack and hooks it back together.

"See?" she says. "It didn't break, it just came apart. It's okay."

He sniffs. She plucks a tissue from a box and hands it to him. "Blow."

In that moment, I glimpse the woman Marin would become. The girl who couldn't sit next to any boy without delivering a jab to the ribs has discovered kindness.

Revenge. She's found it, in the sweetest way.

As the words of "Hamlet" fall from their mouths, these kids get it. They have learned they are capable. Colossal.

In twelfth grade, I couldn't for the life of me make sense of algebra. Why do letters hang out with numbers? I still don't understand it. But I had to pass an exam to graduate, and I was sinking fast until my math teacher, Mr. Campbell, an old softie, knelt beside my desk and talked me through each and every math problem.

"You see, Mr. Campbell," I whispered, "I'm going to be an actress, so I don't really need this."

"I know," he whispered back. "Together, we'll get you graduated, and then you'll go out in the world and do what you have to do."

Thank you, Mr. Campbell.

CHILDREN'S WRITES

I have changed a lot since during the first day of the shakespear club. At first I thought that I was going to mess up and that the performance would be a disaster. But during the middle of shakespear I started to learn my lines. Two weeks before the performance I remembered all of my lines including my big speech. So that made me prepared . . . It is the best club I've ever joined!!

LESSON PLAN

Do it anyway.

ACKNOWLEDGMENTS

'Tis a solitary life, this writing business, but out there are people . . . people without whom I'd surely be lost.

Thank you:

To all those children who trusted me and themselves as we gathered for the Shakespeare Club. I will remember and love every single one of you, forever.

To the wise and dedicated teachers who inspired my self-worth:

MRS. J. SNIDER	MARJ HAHNE
MR. W. CAMPBELL	MARSHA McGREGOR
MR. F. LEPKIN	DOROTHY RANDALL GRAY
MRS. B. WOOLCOMBE	JAN PHILLIPS
MYRA SHAPIRO	ANNE WALRADT
SUSAN TIBERGHIEN	LYNNE BARRETT
EUNICE SCARFE	KURT REIS
JUNE GOULD	UTA HAGEN

For saying "yes" to the Shakespeare Club:

PRINCIPAL YURI HAYASHI-SMITH

To the exceptional teachers who offered classroom tips:

ELVIA PEREZ	KELLI KOZAK
LISA LAICHTMAN	MEREDITH YEH

For taking the Shakespeare Club ride:

LAURA STOCKTON

For his wisdom:

DENNIS PALUMBO

For his inspiration:

ALFRED UHRY

To the early readers of this book:

MAGGIE MARSHALL   B.J. WARD
BOB RUMERMAN   GORDON HUNT
LAURIE HANSEN   MICHELLE FISK

For their East Coast sanctuary:

HEATHER SUMMERHAYES CARIOU
LEN CARIOU

For their enthusiasm:

SCOTT ROZMAN
ERWIN MAAS

To my brothers, fine men both:

TED & MARTY

To my parents, who let me fly.

To CHRISTOPHER ROBBINS, DAVID MILES, MAGGIE WICKES, and the entire
crew at Familius for their enthusiastic and considered embrace of this work.

To my agent, SUSAN SCHULMAN, for her faith and sure-handed guidance.

To WILLIAM YEH, the best of the best, my husband and friend.

ABOUT THE AUTHOR

FOLLOWING A DISTINGUISHED career as a classically trained actor onstage and in film and television, Mel Ryane has found a new artistic home in the written word with her memoir, *Teaching Will: What Shakespeare and 10 Kids Gave Me That Hollywood Couldn't.*

Mel became a professional actor during her teens in her native Canada, then followed her career to New York City and to theatres across North America. After applying her skills to coaching actors on major studio and network projects, Mel was accepted into the Directing Workshop for Women at the prestigious American Film Institute. She subsequently wrote a screenplay that advanced to the semifinal round in the Motion Picture Academy's Nicholl Fellowships in Screenwriting competition.

Mel travels across the country teaching "From Page to Podium: Reading Your Work Aloud," a workshop that helps writers find their public speaking voice. She also offers school workshops introducing Shakespeare to students. She lives Los Angeles with her husband and their dog and cat.

For more information on either program, Mel can be contacted at:
teachingwill@gmail.com

ABOUT FAMILIUS

Welcome to a place where mothers are celebrated, not compared. Where heart is at the center of our families, and family at the center of our homes. Where boo boos are still kissed, cake beaters are still licked, and mistakes are still okay. Welcome to a place where books—and family—are beautiful. Familius: a book publisher dedicated to helping families be happy.

Visit Our Website: www.familius.com

Our website is a different kind of place. Get inspired, read articles, discover books, watch videos, connect with our family experts, download books and apps and audiobooks, and along the way, discover how values and happy family life go together.

Join Our Family

There are lots of ways to connect with us! Subscribe to our newsletters at www.familius.com to receive uplifting daily inspiration, essays from our Pater Familius, a free ebook every month, and the first word on special discounts and Familius news.

Become an Expert

Familius authors and other established writers interested in helping families be happy are invited to join our family and contribute online content. If you have something important to say on the family, join our expert community by applying at:

www.familius.com/apply-to-become-a-familius-expert

Get Bulk Discounts

If you feel a few friends and family might benefit from what you've read, let us know and we'll be happy to provide you with quantity discounts. Simply email us at specialorders@familius.com.

Website: www.familius.com

Facebook: www.facebook.com/paterfamilius

Twitter: @familiustalk, @paterfamilius1

Pinterest: www.pinterest.com/familius

The most important work

you ever do will be within the

walls of your own home.

CPSIA information can be obtained at www.ICGtesting.com
Printed in the USA
BVOW07s1834040814

361135BV00002B/21/P